# Gender Bias, Missing Girls and Population Imbalance

## About the Authors

**Dr. (Mrs.) Sneh Sangwan**, Associate Professor in the Department of Geography, BPSM Girls College, BPS Manila Vishwavidyalaya, Khanpur Kalan (Sonipat), has more than a dozen of research papers and books to her credit. She is a life member of several professional and academic bodies and has participated in more than 25 National and International conferences/seminars/workshops. Dr. Sangwan was unanimously elected as Member of Executive Committee for the two consecutive terms (2003-2005 and 2006-2008) of National Association of Geographers, India (NAGI), which is the **premier academic body** for geographers of India. She has been awarded Major Research Project by UGC as Principal Investigator.

**Prof. Randhir Singh Sangwan,** Professor, at present, working as in the Dept. of Geography, M.D. University, Rohtak, has more than a score of research papers and books to his credit. Prof. Sangwan has participated in more than 50 National and two International Conferences of IGU held at Glasgow, Scotland (Great Britain) and Tunis (Tunisia, Africa) in 2004 and 2008 respectively. Prof. Sangwan received "Prof. R.N. Dubey Memorial Award-2002"—for Academic Excellence in Teaching and Research in Geography. This Award was conferred on by Bhoovigyan Vikas Foundation, the august body of Earth Science Professionals and was presented by the then **His Excellency, Vice President of India.** Dr. Sangwan also held the positions of Vice President and Member, Executive Committee of National Association of Geographers, India (NAGI), New Delhi.

**Mahima**, is a Post Graduate in Geography Department of Geography, Panjab University, Chandigarh. Mahima has a brilliant academic career and is the Gold Medalist of BA (Hons.) Geography from MDU, Rohtak for which State Merit Scholarship was given to her. Mahima did her Post Graduation from Panjab University, Chandigarh and qualified NET for Lectureship in her First attempt in June, 2012. Her active involvement in research activities is just a beginning and, at present, she has only one book and two research papers to her credit.

# Preface

The world, necessarily, seeks to provide a sense of meaning and directions to human existence. This necessitates the understanding of why and what kind of expressions of population are. The human population means a components' synthesis and defines expanding circles of regional identities. Accordingly, region's existence/ identity is inextricably bounded up with the differentials among components of population. A balanced composition of population is alone supposed to ensure an operational identity within local, regional, national and global circles, each of which has its place and value. Population is central to drawing region's identity and the region defines scientific humanism, which means practical and pragmatic, ethical and social altruistic and humanitarian, being governed by practical idealism for social and economic betterment of ecology both natural and human. The human existence represents, in true sense, the synthesis between humanism and scientific accomplishment. The fact of concerns is that every people and every generation suffers from the illusion that their way of looking at things is the only right way or is at any rate, the nearest approach to knowing and realizing the desired result.

Population believes in principle of continuous becoming and an act of growth. However, though powered to think, we fail to feel free to think as we live in a system, in a frame, in a society, in our small hole. We intend to think and act according to the size of our hole, where our consciousness is very limited. We are out of our ignorance. Ignorance keeps us always lonely and worried, confused and frustrated. It forces us to worry and hurry with the question: How to be secure, how to plan and execute? Self-knowledge is, however, different, which removes worry and gives courage, confidence and strength to perform and accomplish right.

It is with the use of our consciousness that we can change. We can choose and refuse to achieve balance through our actions.

This book, entitled "Gender Bias, Missing Girls and Population Imbalance: Regional Concerns and Strategies" is a U.G.C. Major Research Project-related outcome after certain modifications. The subject matter of the book relates to possibly the most dynamic component of population – its sex composition. Possibilities of the human world are always waiting to come out of pious seeds of population sex. It is like the tree in waiting inside the seed to come out. The book is intended to examine differentials in sex composition and to plead for balancing of population sex component with specific reference to the state of Haryana, a federal constituent of the Union of India. To the authors, the awareness to the possibilities, the abilities and the capabilities to ensure balance to human sex components alone will make the regional population useful, meaning and purposeful. Surely, balance is not an attribute of any one component. It is to remember that every component comes in pairs not in terms of opposite, but in terms of ensuring balance in existence.

The book attempts to reveal the growing disparities in social situation in India taking the case of Haryana with reference to sex component of population. Not surprisingly, sex divide, in the context of human population, has formed a research theme of great interest as this divide has influenced, comprehensibly, all other spheres of population composition reflected through select demographic appearances of literate-illiterate, birth-death, emigration-immigration, workers-non-workers and even rural-urban divides. The work has shown the wealth of detailed description and analysis of sex differentials prevalent in the state of Haryana, which is dubiously and frequently referred to have widened the divide. The state has always stood for adverse sex ratio, indicating status of women in the society.

It has to be kept into consideration that the sex ratio status implies an effective index of socio-economic conditions prevailing over some territorial segment and it provides, therefore, useful tools for regional analysis and planning. The sex balance has tended to respond to rural-urban and agro-industrial transformation. The comprehension of regional geography suggests that the trends in socio-economic system of a region become highly responsive to intra-regional changes occurring in sex ratio. The present book

# Gender Bias, Missing Girls and Population Imbalance

## Regional Concerns and Strategies

Sneh Sangwan
Randhir Singh Sangwan
Mahima

**CONCEPT PUBLISHING COMPANY PVT., LTD.**
**NEW DELHI-110059**

**ISBN-13: 978-81-8069-999-3**

First Published 2015

*Published and Printed by*

**Concept Publishing Company Pvt. Ltd.**
A/15-16, Commercial Block, Mohan Garden
New Delhi-110059 (India)
*T*: 25351460, 25351794, *F*: 091-11-25357109
E: publishing@conceptpub.com, W: www.conceptpub.com
**Editorial Office:** H-13, Bali Nagar, New Delhi-110 015, India.

**Cataloging in Publication Data**--Courtesy: D.K. Agencies (P) Ltd. <docinfo@dkagencies.com>

**Sangwan, Sneh,** 1966- **author.**
Gender bias, missing girls and population imbalance : regional concerns and strategies/ Sneh Sangwan, Randhir Singh Sangwan, Mahima.
pages cm
Includes bibliographical references (pages ) and index.
ISBN 9788180699993

1. Sex discrimination against women--India--Haryana. 2. Female feticide--India--Haryana. 3. Sex ratio--India--Haryana. 4. Sex distribution (Demography)--India--Haryana. 5. Girls--India--Haryana--Social conditions. I. Sangwan, Randhir Singh, 1956-, author. II. Mahima, author. III. Title.

DDC 305.420954558 23

# Contents

very succinctly has intended to emphasize the importance of population sex balance in improvement of regional socio-economic systems and to suggest strategies to achieve the same, based on adequate comprehension of conceptual grasp and analytical discourse on socio-economic and demographic characteristics of regional population, perception and awareness among people, issues and concerns of declining sex ratio. It is believed that the coverage of and approach to the study of potent subject matters will provide new insights for all those who are practicing policy and planning for regional development and those students and researchers who are engaged in pursuing study and research in the fields of geography, sociology, economics, psychology, political science and regional economics and analysis.

We are deeply indebted to Bhoogal Ratna Prof. R.P. Misra, Mahatma Gandhi National Fellow and former Vice Chancellor of the University of Allahabad, Allahabad; Prof. B. Thakur, Department of Geography, University of Delhi, Delhi; Prof. Nandeshwar Sharma, former Head, Department of Geography, L.N. Mithila University, Darbhanga; Prof. Suresh Misra, Indian Institute of Public Administration; Prof. S.P. Sinha, former Chairman, Department of Geography, Kurukshetra University, Kurukshetra; Dr. R.B. Singh, Associate Professor, Department of Geography, University of Delhi, Delhi; Sh. S.C. Gupta, Principal (Retd.), Department of Geography, Government P.G. College, Jhajjar; for their valuable suggestions, encouragement and unstinted moral support in completing the work.

We would like to place on record our deep sense of gratitude to all those officers/officials of various departments belonging to Government of Haryana as well as Government of India for the help and cooperation they extended whenever we visited their offices. We express our gratitude especially to Dr. Narveer Singh, Director General of Health Services, Haryana, Chandigarh for the help and cooperation, he extended whenever we visited his office. We also express our thanks to Civil Surgeons and other staff members of the concerned Community Health Centres and Primary Health Centres for their help provided in the collection of data. Anganwadi workers of the Target Villages deserve special thanks for their cooperation in conducting the Field Survey.

We express our thanks to all the respondents in the study areas of the target villages, without their cooperation and involvement; we would not have completed this task.

We are also grateful to the staff members of the libraries of Maharshi Dayanand University, Rohtak; Jawahar Lal Nehru University, New Delhi; University of Delhi (Ratan Tata Library), Delhi; and Panjab University, Chandigarh. We also owe our gratitude to various authors whose works have been consulted and quoted in the present study.

Our indebtedness is due towards our family members, especially our children Mahima Sangwan and Himanshu Sangwan, who were caring and resourceful in all our endeavours. All our near and dear ones who helped us in any manner also deserve our thanks.

We also acknowledge the keen interest and dedication with which Mr. Rakesh Sangwan of Computer Zone, Rohtak and Ms. Anita typed the manuscript.

It would be highly gratifying for us if our humble effort proves to be thought provoking and opens up new vistas.

We take the opportunity to express our special thanks to Shri Ashok Kumar Mittal, Concept Publishing Company Pvt. Ltd., New Delhi for readily agreeing to publish this book and bringing it out expeditiously and efficiently.

For a few errors that may have crept into the book, we crave the indulgence of readers and own sole responsibility.

Above all, we remember God almighty for the abundant blessings bestowed on us without which we would not have completed this work.

**Sneh Sangwan**
**Randhir Singh Sangwan**
**Mahima**

# List of Maps



# List of Figures

# List of Tables

# 1 Introduction

Population sex balance has remained a relevant research theme of significant interest in many fields of social sciences including Geography. It implies the explanations of the commonality and complexities of the spatial process of human dispersal and adaptation. The process of early humanization of the Earth through human diffusion, by today's standards began to mark a very slow and common process. The process involved interplay and experimentation with the conditions prevailing in bioclimatic habitats. The regional population continued to expand in number and area through a variety of technologies. Population composition too did not remain static and the problem of imbalances in its components has shown the tendency of persistence and aggravation.

The problem of imbalance in sex ratio has been found to persist since long and seems to aggravate anew as ever before. The origin of the research problem lies, though, in the cultural components of humanity which exerts an important role in patterning of population, but it advances to aggravate with changes in demographic trends that have continued to evolve over long period of time.

No element is considered more central to the study of population problems than the context and setting of sex component. Male-female composition and its status of balance express all pervasive dimensions of human world. Sex ratio in India in general and in Haryana in particular, has adverse inheritance right from the beginning of census records completion. Disproportionate share between male and female components of population has released problems of socio-economic implications, because sex ratio has been considered an index of socio-economic conditions of an area and a useful tool of regional analysis. The problem of imbalances in population, sex is compounded by the fact that sex ratio, in itself, is a function of factors like sex ratio at birth (SRB), differential in mortality of the males and females and sex-selectivity among the migrants.

## 1.1 Framing the Research Problem

Since, the inception of human being, male and female both are essential components of a society for healthy growth. In some societies, females are more than males and in some males are more than females. This creates imbalance and becomes cause of many social problems.

In our country, sex ratio always remained in favour of males due to various causes. Now the situation has worsened in almost all the States and Union Territories especially in developed states. Despite the fact that Haryana is a well-developed state, it is facing the problem of excessive deficiency of females (861 females per thousand males). Haryana with 819 females per thousand males is next to Punjab (798 females per thousand males) in terms of the lowest child sex ratio as per 2001 census which seems to be the result of the increasing incidence of female foeticide particularly among literate population in urban areas because of awareness and easy access to sex selective technology.

Increasing gap between two sexes is becoming a major cause of many social problems like increase in crime rate, rapes, domestic violence, trafficking in girls as brides from backward states through the process of *buying and selling* of brides, etc.

Though, due to the efforts of the government as well as by various social groups and NGOs, Haryana has experienced a marginal increase in case of over-all sex ratio (from 861 in 2001 to 877 in 2011) and child sex ratio (from 819 in 2001 to 830 in 2011), but still it is at the lowest rung of ladder amongst the states of India. So, the population sex balance has become a burning and relevant research theme of Population Geographers today in case of Haryana. Being a population geographer, I find it essential to trace the underlying causes of this increasing imbalance in sex ratio especially in 0-6 age-group. In this age-group, the situation is drastic and can break up the social values and social structure in future. So, the need of the hour is to find out the ways for balancing the sex components.

## 1.2 Research Theme Coverage

The theme coverage of the present research work relates to the issues of the investigation into the nature, degree and direction of child sex ratio in time and place dimension.

### *1.2.1 Objectives*

The present research project is aimed at balancing population sex components in Haryana. Haryana is a state with excessive deficiency of females and is characterized with the lowest sex ratio of 861 females per thousand males amongst various states of India as per 2001 census. The sex ratio has been on a continuous decline since the beginning of 20th century with only some nominal exceptions.

The research project proposes to outline the following important objectives:

(i) To give a temporal analysis of changing sex ratio since 1901.
(ii) To know about the prevailing social attitude of people responsible for the increasing incidence of female foeticide in Haryana.
(iii) To find out various causes responsible for the increasing incidence of female foeticide resulting into missing unborn girls in Haryana.
(iv) To explain the socio-cultural implications because of missing unborn girls due to increasing trend of female foeticide in the patriarchal (male-dominated) society of Haryana.
(v) To give a list of various remedial measures to control the increasing incidence of female foeticide resulting into missing unborn girls in Haryana.

## 1.3 Research Area Coverage

The necessity of the theme to be carried out in some area

perspective makes it imperative to locate some area coverage of the research. The research work selects the state of Haryana to form its universe of study (Map 1.1).

Haryana state came into existence as an independent state on 1st November 1966, after the reorganization of composite state of Punjab on linguistic basis. It is located in north-western part of India (Map 1.1). It stretches from 27°38′N to 30°55′5″ N latitudes and from 74°27′ 8″ east to 77°36′5″ E longitudes. It is bounded by the orchard state of Himachal Pradesh in the north and north-east; by Uttar Pradesh, the most populous state and Union Territory of Delhi in the east; and by the Union Territory of Chandigarh and Punjab, the state of adventurist farmers and toiling workers, in its north-west. Rajasthan with its rich cultural heritage and history replete with most heroic deeds bounds the state of Haryana on south and south-west.

The administrative boundaries of Haryana state have been changed from time to time due to the political conditions but the geographical and natural boundaries of the state have remained the same. Geographically, the boundaries of Haryana state are found in river Ghaggar in the north-west, Siwalik hills in the north-east, River Yamuna in the east, Aravali hills in the south and the Thar Desert in the south-west.

Haryana is one of the smaller states of India. According to Census of India (2001), the area of the state is 44,212 km$^2$ and is inhabited by 211.45 lakh persons. The area and population of the state constitute 1.35 and 1.93 per cent of the total area and population of India respectively. Thus, Haryana ranks 17th in terms of area and 16th in population size among the 28 states and 7 Union Territories in 2001 census. The administrative division of Haryana comprises 19 districts and 67 tehsils as per 2001 census (Map 1.1).

## 1.4 Research Methodological Approach

### *1.4.1 Research Methodology*

The present research work rely partly on theoretical and largely on empirical methodology to arrive at the desired results. Intensive survey on the basis of well prepared schedule has been made to collect information regarding the demographic and socio-economic characteristics of people residing in rural Haryana. The facts and

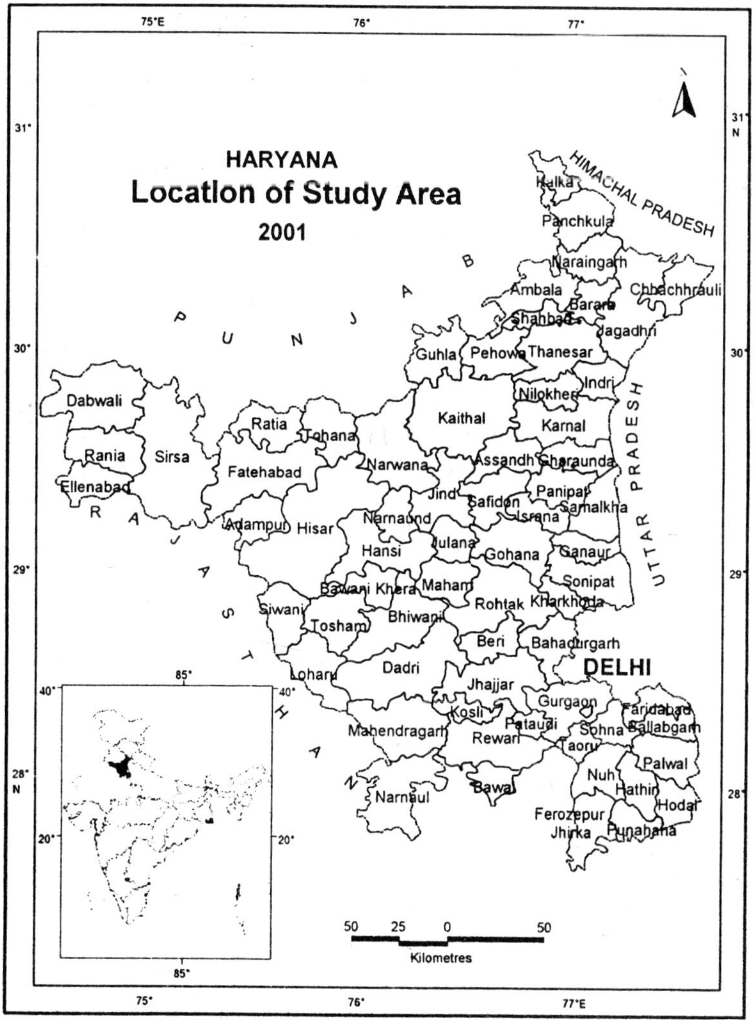


**Map 1.1:** Haryana: Location of Study Area (2001)

figures collected by Field Survey have been analyzed comprehensibly and use of statistical and cartographic techniques and preparation of maps has assisted the geographic spirit of study. The methodological base of the present research work involves thus, the trio of acquisitive, diagnostic and prescriptive ways to the completion of research work.

**Table 1.1:** Haryana: Facts Summary, 2001 and 2011

| Sr. No. | State/District | Population | | | Per cent Decadal Growth Rate of Population | | Sex Ratio | | Density of Population | |
|---|---|---|---|---|---|---|---|---|---|---|
| | | Persons | Males | Females | 1991-2001 | 2001-2011 | 2001 | 2011 | 2001 | 2011 |
| | **Haryana** | **25353081** | **13505130** | **11847951** | **28.43** | **19.90** | **861** | **877** | **478** | **573** |
| 1. | Panchkula | 558890 | 298919 | 259971 | 50.91 | 19.32 | 823 | 870 | 522 | 622 |
| 2. | Ambala | 1136784 | 604044 | 532740 | 25.78 | 12.06 | 868 | 882 | 644 | 722 |
| 3. | Yamuna Nagar | 1214162 | 646801 | 567361 | 29.19 | 16.56 | 862 | 877 | 589 | 687 |
| 4. | Kurukshetra | 964231 | 510370 | 453861 | 23.32 | 16.81 | 866 | 889 | 540 | 630 |
| 5. | Kaithal | 1074861 | 570595 | 502266 | 21.02 | 13.39 | 853 | 880 | 408 | 463 |
| 6. | Karnal | 1506323 | 798840 | 707483 | 23.06 | 18.22 | 865 | 886 | 506 | 598 |
| 7. | Panipat | 1202811 | 646324 | 556487 | 38.58 | 24.33 | 829 | 861 | 763 | 949 |
| 8. | Sonipat | 1480080 | 798948 | 681132 | 22.39 | 15.71 | 839 | 853 | 603 | 697 |
| 9. | Jind | 1332042 | 712254 | 619788 | 21.36 | 11.95 | 852 | 870 | 440 | 493 |
| 10. | Fatehabad | 941522 | 494834 | 446688 | 24.76 | 16.79 | 884 | 903 | 318 | 371 |
| 11. | Sirsa | 1295114 | 683242 | 611872 | 23.59 | 15.98 | 882 | 896 | 961 | 303 |
| 12. | Hisar | 1742815 | 931535 | 811280 | 27.11 | 13.38 | 851 | 871 | 386 | 438 |
| 13. | Bhiwani | 1629109 | 864616 | 764493 | 22.49 | 14.32 | 879 | 884 | 298 | 341 |
| 14. | Rohtak | 1058683 | 566708 | 491975 | 21.00 | 12.61 | 847 | 888 | 539 | 607 |
| 15. | Jhajjar | 956907 | 514303 | 442604 | 23.06 | 8.73 | 847 | 861 | 480 | 522 |
| 16. | Mahendragarh | 921680 | 486553 | 435127 | 19.16 | 13.43 | 918 | 894 | 428 | 485 |
| 17. | Rewari | 896129 | 472254 | 423875 | 25.34 | 17.09 | 899 | 898 | 480 | 562 |
| 18. | Gurgaon | 1514085 | 817274 | 696811 | 44.15 | 73.93 | 850 | 853 | 717 | 1241 |
| 19. | Mewat | 1089406 | 571480 | 517926 | 45.67 | 37.94 | 899 | 906 | 526 | 729 |
| 20. | Faridabad | 1798954 | 961532 | 837422 | 58.88 | 31.75 | 826 | 871 | 1744 | 2298 |
| 21. | Palwal | 1040493 | 553704 | 486789 | 34.21 | 25.49 | 862 | 879 | 606 | 761 |

*Source:* Census of India (2011), *Provisional Population Totals*, Paper-1 of 2011, Haryana, Series 7, Director of Census Operations, Haryana.

As the study refers to the spatial analysis of child sex ratio of rural Haryana, the tehsil has been considered to be the most suitable unit of study. There are 67 tehsils in Haryana as per 2001 census.

In every geographic inquiry, spatial concept occupies the central position in its methodology where the preparation of a map is the most important tool. A map showing district and tehsil boundaries were obtained from census publications.

### 1.4.2 Data Base

The project involves both primary and secondary data. However, the reference year for the secondary data is 2001, but the provisional data for 2011 census have also been incorporated subject to requirement and availability of data published so far. The secondary data have been obtained from the following sources:

*Census of India Publications*

- Primary Census Abstract, General Population
- General Population Tables and Primary Census Abstract
- Social and Cultural Tables
- Special Tables on Scheduled Castes
- Census Atlas
- Sample Registration System Statistical Reports
- SRS Bulletins
- SRS Based Abridged Life Tables
- Census CDs

*Haryana Government Publications*

- Statistical Abstract of Haryana
- Economic Survey of Haryana
- District Census Handbooks for each District
- Occasional Papers published by Directorate of Census Operations, Haryana, Chandigarh and office of the Registrar General and Census Commissioner, New Delhi
- Provisional Population Totals, Papers-1 and 2 of 2011.

*Publications Made by Economic Intelligence Service*

- Basic Statistics Relating to the Indian Economy, States,

2 Tables 2.1 and 2.4, Centre for Monitoring Indian Economy Pvt. Ltd., New Delhi.

- Profile of States, Centre for Monitoring Indian Economy Pvt. Ltd., New Delhi.
- The primary data have, however, been generated at the level of villages. The units of analysis are both Villages and Tehsils.
- The primary data have been collected through *interview schedules*. The respondents were selected randomly from villages, keeping in view the proportion of different castes in the village.

### 1.4.3 Survey Design

*Sample Size*

An important issue in any survey design is the determination of sample size. However, five major factors, i.e. cost, time, geography, level of accuracy, and sub-group analysis, play a role in the determination of sample size, but the major factor considered is the selection of a desired accuracy level for the survey results. The sample size necessary to achieve such a result in case of present study has been computed to be 11,357 households out of the total universe of 56,934 households. The village-wise *sampling fraction* (the percentage of the population to be interviewed) is given in Tables 1.2 and 1.3.

*Sampling Frame*

Prior to selecting a sample, the *population* or *universe* to which inference will be made must be defined. As we have to calculate the child sex ratio of rural areas of Haryana, a list or *sampling frame* is needed of all the sampling units (households) within this population. In some cases, this is a simple task, but in many cases, the development of a sampling frame is a tedious process. Geographers are often interested in drawing a random sample of all residents of a city, yet no sampling frame exists for such a population (Sheskin, 1987).

In the present study, the 2001 census list of villages served as the *sampling frame*.

*Sampling Unit*

Household is taken as the unit of sampling in order to collect relevant data.

*Sampling Approach*

There are two types of survey sampling approaches—probability and non-probability. Probability sampling designs have been widely used in geographic research. Because, if one wants to make inferences about the total population from which the sample is drawn, it cannot be done unless one uses a *probability sampling design*. Hence, in the present study, *two-stage random sampling design* was adopted to make the same a true representative of the population.

The first stage involved selection of Primary Sampling Units (PSUs), i.e., villages, with probability proportional to population size (PPS). A total of 21 villages were selected (Table 1.2) which were having child sex ratio below 750 females per 1000 males and the population (in 0-6 age-group) above 1000. Keeping in view the time constraint, it was not possible to make survey of all the villages (161) attributed with child sex ratio below 750 females per 1000 males. Hence, at second stage, we have selected 36 villages (Table 1.3) which were having juvenile sex ratio below 700 females per 1000 males and the population (in 0-6 age-group) between 500 and 1000. At both stages, a twenty per cent sample from each village was taken.

While taking sample, the caste structure of the concerned village was also kept in mind so that it may be best representative of all the castes. As the survey was conducted during day, in many instances, only female respondents were available for interaction. Wherever possible, couples were interviewed together at their home. Even when, the husband or wife was interviewed separately, the data and information collected pertains to the entire household.

### 1.4.4 Mode of Survey Data Collection

However, there are many *modes of survey data collection,* but the face-to-face (or in-house) interviewing is the most flexible and reliable method in survey research. Here, in the present study, the Project Fellow goes to the primary sampling unit (e.g. household), talks to the chosen person within it, and conducts the interview

**Table 1.2:** Haryana: Sampling Fraction by Villages i.e. No. of Villages Selected for Survey with Population (0-6) Above 1000 and Sex Ratio (0-6) Below 750 (2001)

| *Sr. No.* | *State/Tehsil* | *Village* | *Sex Ratio (0-6)* | *No. of Households* | *Sample Size (20%)* |
|---|---|---|---|---|---|
| | **Haryana** | | **819** | **2541980** | |
| 1. | Panchkula | Barwala | 742 | 1313 | 262 |
| 2. | Shahbad | Ismailabad | **678** | 2184 | **436** |
| 3. | Kaithal | Habri | 732 | 1897 | 378 |
| 4. | Karnal | Singoha | 742 | 1014 | 202 |
| 5. | Israna | Naultha | 743 | 1436 | 286 |
| 6. | Gohana | Dhanana Aladadpur | 724 | 1087 | 216 |
| 7. | Kharkhoda | Rohna | **711** | 1345 | **269** |
| 8. | Jind | Dauhla | 744 | 1371 | 274 |
| 9. | Sirsa | Ding | 723 | 1403 | 280 |
| 10. | Rania | Jiwan Nagar | 735 | 2196 | 438 |
| 11. | Hisar | Satrod Kalan | 733 | 2279 | 454 |
| 12. | Maham | Lakhan Majra | 749 | 1641 | 328 |
| 13. | Rohtak | Hassangarh | 726 | 1229 | 244 |
| 14. | Beri | Majra | 735 | 1466 | 292 |
| 15. | Bahadurgarh | Badli | **716** | 2608 | **520** |
| 16. | Jhajjar | Matanhail | 725 | 1302 | 260 |
| 17. | Gurgaon | Kadipur (Part) | 745 | 1677 | 334 |
| 18. | Palwal | Alawalpur | 750 | 1235 | 247 |
| 19. | Palwal | Dhatir | 742 | 1086 | 217 |
| 20. | Palwal | Janauli | 730 | 904 | 180 |
| 21. | Hodal | Pingor | 731 | 856 | 170 |
| | **Total Households** | | | **31,529** | **6,287** |

*Source:* Census of India (2001), *Primary Census Abstract*, CDs 1-12, Office of the Registrar General and Census Commissioner, India, New Delhi.

face-to-face. In the diversified population of Haryana, it was decided to adopt *interview-schedule* as the mode for collecting survey data and it was canvassed by the investigator himself.

### *1.4.5 Field Experiences*

In canvassing the interview schedule in the field of study, the following situations were encountered by the investigator who adopted the following course of action after taking into account the possible alternatives:

(i) As indicated earlier, the head of the household was taken

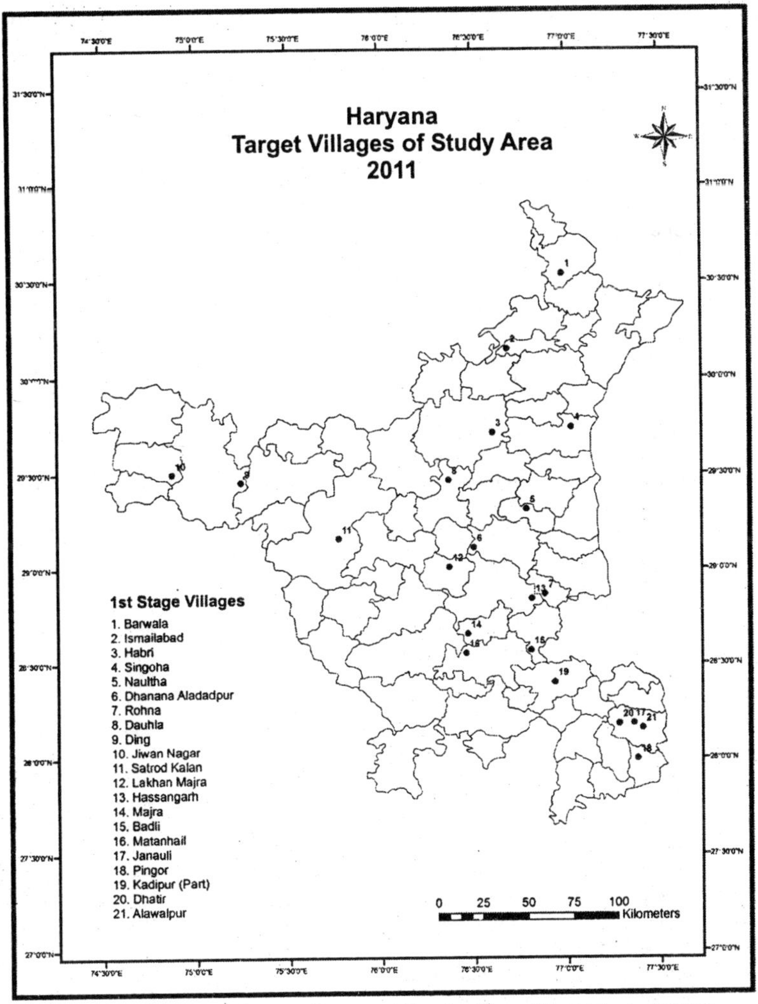


**Map 1.2:** Haryana: Target Villages of Study Area, First Stage (2011)

as the respondent. In case of his non-availability, the spouse was interviewed. In rare cases, an educated member of the household was used as an interpreter when the head was not able to comprehend all the questions.

(ii) In a few cases, the identity of the investigator was suspected to be a doctor from Family Planning Department and sometimes as an income-tax officer. A lot of time was

**Table 1.3:** Haryana: Sampling Fraction by Villages, i.e. No. of Villages Selected for Survey with Population Between 500-1000 and Sex Ratio (0-6) Below 700 (2001)

| Sr. No. | State/Tehsil | Village | Sex Ratio (0-6) | No. of House-holds | Sample Size (20%) |
|---|---|---|---|---|---|
| | **Haryana** | | **819** | **25,41,980** | |
| 1 | Panchkula | Garhi | 695 | 598 | 120 |
| 2 | Naraingarh | Kurali | 647 | 657 | 131 |
| 3 | Naraingarh | Majra | 597 | 740 | 148 |
| 4 | Ambala | Shahpur | 612 | 860 | 172 |
| 5 | Ambala | Singanwala (Part) | 601 | 763 | 152 |
| 6 | Shahbad | Jhansa | 694 | 1094 | 219 |
| 7 | Shahbad | Nalwi | 667 | 674 | 135 |
| 8 | Pehowa | Thaska Miranji | 688 | 697 | 139 |
| 9 | Guhla | Balbehra | 686 | 702 | 140 |
| 10 | Guhla | Kheri Gulamali | 651 | 624 | 125 |
| 11 | Kaithal | Sangri | 669 | 580 | 116 |
| 12 | Gharaunda | Phurlak | 682 | 586 | 117 |
| 13 | Gharaunda | Pabana Hassanpur | 666 | 562 | 112 |
| 14 | Panipat | Babail | 697 | 959 | 192 |
| 15 | Samalkha | Dehra | 685 | 688 | 137 |
| 16 | Sonipat | Nahri | 695 | 1244 | 249 |
| 17 | Sonipat | Barwasni | 665 | 865 | 163 |
| 18 | Sonipat | Karar Ibrahimpur | 632 | 616 | 123 |
| 19 | Kharkhoda | Bidhlan | 654 | 585 | 117 |
| 20 | Kharkhoda | Thana Kalan | 650 | 721 | 144 |
| 21 | Tohana | Pirthla | 696 | 630 | 126 |
| 22 | Sirsa | Rupawas | 670 | 537 | 107 |
| 23 | Sirsa | Darbi | 655 | 702 | 140 |
| 24 | Sirsa | Jhorar Nali | 639 | 938 | 188 |
| 25 | Sirsa | Nattar | 613 | 644 | 129 |
| 26 | Hisar | Sarsana | 692 | 265 | 53 |
| 27 | Bahadurgarh | Kharhar | 699 | 999 | 200 |
| 28 | Bahadurgarh | Jakhauda | 678 | 630 | 126 |
| 29 | Jhajjar | Machhrauli | 678 | 668 | 134 |
| 30 | Mahendragarh | Sehlang | 637 | 874 | 175 |
| 31 | Narnaul | Kanwariawas | 666 | 584 | 117 |
| 32 | Rewari | Dhawana | 686 | 633 | 127 |
| 33 | Rewari | Bharawas | 669 | 714 | 143 |
| 34 | Rewari | Lisan | 604 | 641 | 128 |
| 35 | Sohna | Rethoj | 700 | 545 | 109 |
| 36 | Hodal | Jatoli | 700 | 586 | 117 |
| | **Total Household** | | | **25,405** | **5,070** |

*Source:* Census of India (2001), *Primary Census Abstract*, CDs 1-12, Office of the Registrar General and Census Commissioner, India, New Delhi.

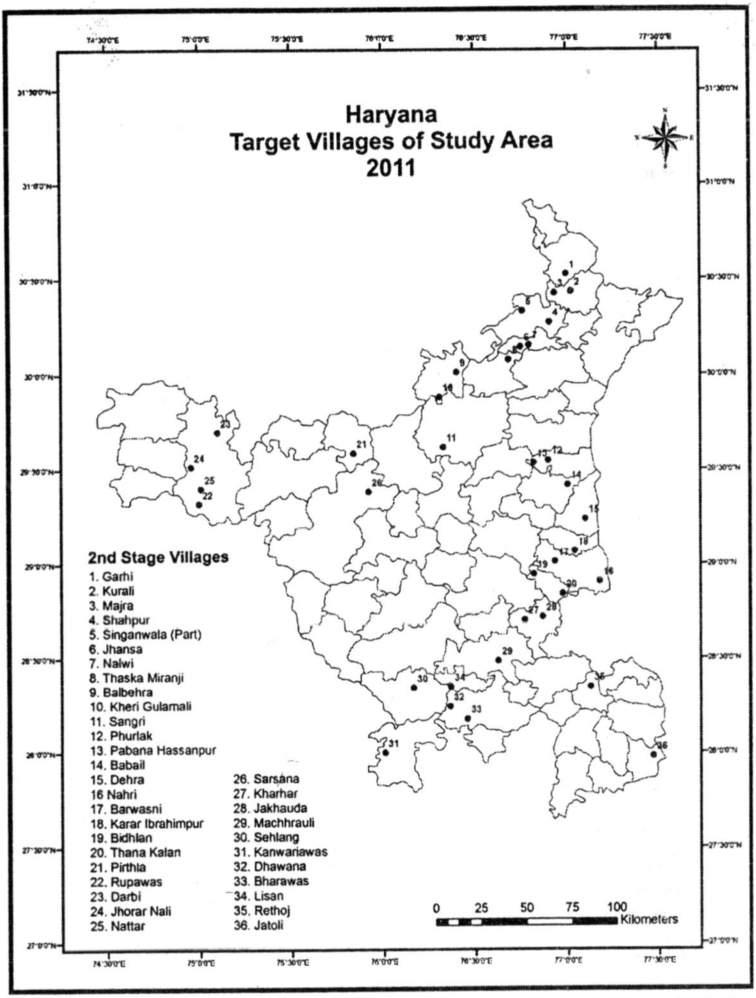


**Map 1.3:** Haryana: Target Villages of Study Area, Second Stage (2011)

wasted in such cases to satisfy the respondents by showing the university identity card and the letter of authority either on behalf of the Principal Investigator or the Principal of the college concerned.

(iii) On the whole, the respondents were cooperative and willingly agreed to respond. In a few quarrelsome cases, the patience of the investigator saved the situation.

### 1.5 Significance of the Study

The significance of the present research project lies in the fact that it has brought to light the regional variations in child sex ratio and sex disparity among the various segments of population in Haryana. The identification of such variations is only possible if the problem is analysed spatially both at micro and meso levels.

So, at meso level, the tehsil has been chosen as the unit of analysis to explain the spatial patterns of child sex ratio and its differentials in Haryana. At micro level, however, some of the critical villages from various tehsils have been selected as sample villages.

When we are aware of the gravity of problem in terms of regional imbalances, only then solutions could be found out towards the balancing of sex components.

Hence, the present research project has become necessity of a state like Haryana which has been attributed with a highly skewed child sex ratio and every section of society feels concerned about it.

The results and suggestions of this research work can be implemented in other states also to balance the sex components in the country as a whole.

### 1.6 Interdisciplinary Relevance

Population study may, though, be understood to be preserve of not anyone discipline, yet it suggests study material/themes of interdisciplinary concerns. The study of social sciences is inherently, attached to aspects directly related to population/group of people and human pursuits and activities at large. Sociology claims to analyse social organizational and behavioural attributes of population. Population forms the fundamental inputs of historical, economic and political sciences. Geography considers population as its reference element of study in its temporal and spatial dimensions.

The comprehension and research related to sex balance provide inputs to acknowledge the employment and consumption patterns, social needs and pursuits, human psychology and behavioural and spatial patterns of population. The relevance of the present research has, thus, no disciplinary boundaries and merits recognition as essential subject matters of research in social sciences having interdisciplinary implications. To its inherent character, the issues of population sex balance is fundamental to the geographic analysis of a region, for they are not only important features of the cultural landscape, but also influence the other demographic elements significantly and as such provide additional means and materials for analyzing entire regional landscape.

## 1.7 Potential Contribution to Knowledge in the Field of Social Relevance or National Importance

Do not count population. Count upon them. One billion cross people. Are they a liability? Or can they be turned into national asset? If they can be made asset, how can they be? It's a billion count questions. National human resource evolves out of biological reproduction, which represents the essential function of balancing act of two sexes of population. The adverse balance of sex ratio in favour of male segment of population symbolizes the suppressed status of women in society. Wide regional differences in sex ratio have tended to widen or narrow down. Trends in socio-economic life of a region intend to establish corresponding relationship with changes in balance in sex ratio. Haryana represents unique state in terms of sex balance highly unfavourable to women section of society.

Implications of declining sex ratio (numbers of females per thousand males) has become a grave national concern of social and economic relevance. The present research intends to focus on relevant convictions that male selectivity; both with reference to child preference at birth and rural-urban migration has proved to be root cause of imbalance in sex ratio and the situation is bound to turn detrimental to social and economic organizational empowerment and equity. The relevance of the assertion that empower the people, especially the young ones, and they will take care of themselves, will only be supported by the conclusion that balancing population sex components will alone provide base and force of human resource for social and economic strength of the nation.

# 2 Review of Research and Development in the Subject

The steadily widening gap between two components of population (i.e. deteriorating sex ratio) over the last one hundred years and particularly since the beginning of the current century presents an alarming situation. A number of eminent scholars, during the second half of twentieth century, have focused their attention towards this widening gap between two sex components of various populations. So, to address this issue, the studies conducted by various scholars are focused either on sex ratio or on female foeticide or female discrimination or missing girls or sex-selective abortions.

## 2.1 Studies on Sex Ratio

Sex ratio studies can be accounted in the names of Trewartha (1953), Franklin (1956), Clarke (1960, 1972), Lall (1962), Shyrock (1976), Sinha (1979), Misra (1980), and Chandna (1986). All of them have studied sex ratio in various countries and made comparisons among them. A few of them have also studied the sex ratio of world as well as Indian sex ratio and explained that the sex ratio in the developed world is in favour of females, while it is in favour of males in the less developed and developing world, India being in the latter.

Several studies at national level based on the census data were carried out by various researchers. Gosal (1961), Visaria (1971), Natrajan (1971), Premi (2001), etc. have investigated into sex ratio in detail for India. These studies were based on census data and had demographic approach. They have given a generalized explanation on the distribution of sex composition trends and factor affecting sex composition. They concluded that sex ratio is affected by mainly four factors, i.e. sex ratio at birth, migration, differential mortality in male and female and undercounting of females in the census. They also discussed pattern in sex ratio in India and highlighted the associated factors.

Despite the literature-boom concerning sex composition at the Global level (Trewartha, 1953; Franklin, 1956; Clark, 1960, 1972; Shyrock, 1976), National level (Gosal, 1961; Desai, 1967; Bose *et al.*, 1977; Mitra, 1979; Bose, 1991; Senapati, 1993; and Bhutani, 1995; Reddy, 1996; Agnihotri, 2000; Gosal, 2001; and Sangwan and Sangwan, 2003), and State level (Siddiqui and Ahmad, 1971; Chandna, 1972; Krishan and Chandna, 1973; Kashyap, 1975; Siddiqui, 1982; Mehta and Kaur, 1983; Borooah, 1985; Gill and Singh, 1985; Maurya and Devi, 1985; Prasad, 1990; Bose, 1991; Jayasree and Audinarayana, 1991), the notable contributions made by geographers regarding sex composition of Haryana are a few to count and mainly belong to Siddiqui and Ahmad, 1971; Chandna, 1972; Krishan and Chandna, 1973; George and Dahiya, 1998; Gill, 2000; Hassan, 2000 and 2002; Unisa *et al.* (2007); and Sangwan and Sangwan, 2008.

### *2.1.1 National-Level Studies*

In India, some studies were conducted at the national scale. Gosal (1961) observed that the rural-urban differences in sex ratio are of tremendous importance because the sex ratio is lower in towns than in villages. He found that rural-urban differential in sex ratio was just opposite to that in the United States and Western Europe. Desai (1967) found that variations in sex ratio have been conspicuous between rural and urban sub-groups of population. Chandna and Sidhu (1979) studied the sex ratio and its determinants. Mitra (1979) examined the implications of declining sex ratio in India's population by rural-urban residence. Senapati (1993) has focused on trends and implications of sex ratio in India. Bhutani (1995) has discussed rural-urban sex ratio and the change in it over a decade, i.e. 1971-81. Reddy (1996) presents a view of the declining trend of sex ratio in India.

The spatial pattern of sex ratio in India is marked with a sharp divide between the north and western states, on the one hand,

and the rest of the country, on the other. Referred to as the north-south dichotomy in the sex composition of India's population, the topic has also occupied the attention of the scholars. This dichotomy refers to a great deficit of females in the northern states as compared to southern states of the country.

Sopher (1980) has argued that the north-south difference in sex ratio is due to social institution having ecological basis. He has also analyzed the sex ratio of Hindu and Muslim population using state-wise data as a part of chapter, entitled 'Cultural Pattern of India'. The concept of 'north-south' divide is also noticed in the workers of scholars belonging to other disciplines in social sciences (Bardhan, 1974; Visaria, 1971).

Miller (1981) in her book on '*The Endangered Sex*' examined the various approaches to sex composition in India, in general and in the rural areas of the north-western states, in particular. She blamed culture rather than nature on neglect of female children in the region and called it as *culture against females*. She worked out the interaction between the needs of agricultural production, the nature of property holding and the sexual profile of the population. According to Miller, the future of females in India may be further endangered by increasing possibilities of sex selection of offspring at the time of conception (Bardhan, 1982). She has highlighted the differences in the nature of gender relations between propertied classes and 'others' implying that in the latter sex ratio is higher than among the former. Subsequently, in another study, Miller (1989) analysed the regional patterns in juvenile sex ratio in rural India using 1961 and 1971 data in terms of changes in mortality differentials between boys and girls.

Nearly two decades earlier, Krishnaji (1987) has attempted to explain the link between poverty and sex ratio. His work is not directly concerned with the factors behind the level and the declining trend in the sex ratio. Instead he attempted to examine the link between differentials in mortality and imbalance between the sexes on the one hand, and poverty, on the other, in rural households. Thus, as an indirect inference, he argues that the sex ratios are more imbalanced among households with large land-holding—even in south India where sex ratios are more evenly balanced than among agricultural labourers or small cultivators.

Agnihotri (1995, 1996, 2000) gave emphasis on disaggregated analysis of sex ratio for SC/ST and rest of the population. He analysed age-wise sex ratio in detail. He argued that the overall trend of declining FMR is not uniform across the country, but varies from one region to another and by social status, age group and levels of prosperity.

In a latest study, Agnihotri (2003) comments that 'sociological and anthropological literature provide many instances of increased female subordination among the more prosperous groups.

Using NSSO data of 43rd to 50th rounds, Sidhantha *et al.* (2003) have shown a declining trend of sex ratio with rise in prosperity level. For prosperity, the authors have used average monthly per capita expenditure (AMPCE) as a measure of prosperity level. They argue that the inverse association between prosperity level and sex ratio is more pronounced for the later rounds of the NSSO.

Dreze and Sen (2004) analysed female-male ratio in India in an article on "Gender Inequality and Women Agency" under various heads as female-male ratio, gender and caste, child mortality, widowhood and gender relation, gender equality and social problems. This is a demographic analysis based on census data for the period 1901-1991 focused on age-specific female-male ratio, literacy, growth rate of population and infant mortality.

### 2.1.2 *State-Level Studies*

At state level, the studies on sex ratio have been conducted by Siddiqui and Ahmad (1971), Chandna (1972), Krishan and Chandna (1973), Kashyap (1975), Siddiqui (1982), Mehta and Kaur (1983), Borooah (1985), Gill and Singh (1985), Maurya and Devi (1985), Prasad (1990), Bose (1991), Jayasree and Audinarayana (1991), Sangwan and Sangwan (2008). The areas of interest have been the states of Haryana, Punjab, Uttar Pradesh, Rajasthan, Assam, West Bengal and Tamil Nadu. The maximum focus has been on the state of Haryana followed by Punjab.

Chandna and Krishan (1973) explained sex composition of Haryana's population on the basis of census data during 1901-1971. They found that unlike other states in the country, Haryana is characterized by a high sex ratio in rural areas than in the urban areas.

Kaur and Sultana (2004), while examining declining sex ratio in Punjab, argue that son preference is deeply embedded in the socio-cultural ethos, economic needs, and religious ceremonies.

They gave examples of folk songs, proverbs, common sayings and folktales from Punjabi culture related to soon preference in Punjab.

### 2.2 Studies on Son Preference

Williamson (1978) analyzed the problem from the cultural viewpoint on the preference for boys and girls. He argued that the choice of son is universal except in few societies. He has examined the social, economic, psychological and demographic implication of preferring either sex. His work is a brief theoretical analysis of the human sex preferences and control.

Raju and Bhat (1995) analyzed the sex composition of living children associated with socio-economic factors while studying their relative influence on the acceptance of family planning methods and found that more than 85 per cent of the women with at least one son and daughter(s) had accepted family planning methods. The most unfavourable sex composition of living children, for couples not accepting family planning methods, with no son and only daughters, or one son and no daughter.

### 2.3 Studies on Missing Girls

Barbara Miller (1981), in her pioneering anthropological study of the neglect of female children in north India, illustrated the strong relationship between culture and mortality. It is the cultural bias against females in north India, which brings into play neglect and mistreatment of unknown numbers of girl children. According to her, the solution to this problematic future lies "in giving high priority to achieving gender equality in economic entitlement and increased awareness of the social importance of equal health and survival of males and female" (Miller, 1981: 214).

In a significant article titled as "More than 100 million Women are Missing", Amartya Sen (1990) brought to focus on the increasing gender discrimination by analyzing the male-female ratio. He argued rather convincingly that the problem of missing women is clearly one of the momentous and neglected problems facing the world today.

Mari Bhat (2000, 2002) gave a detailed account of 'missing females' in India. He adopted various demographic techniques to solve the puzzle of the missing females. In his disaggregated analysis, based on data for various age-groups, for geographic regions and for different social groups, he gave different clues on declining sex ratio in India. Mari Bhat argues that improvement in the quality of age data on children can produce spurious trend of falling sex ratio at certain childhood ages.

Sangwan and Sangwan (2008), while analyzing the skewed juvenile sex ratio in Haryana and the causes responsible for it, emphasized that because of patriarchal society of Haryana, son preference is the root cause of missing girls in the state due to female foeticide through sex-selective abortions which led to an alarming fall in child ratio. The situation has worsened since 1991, particular in the 0-6 age-group. Census 2001 figures showed that the child sex ratio, which land become a concern in the 1991 census, has gone down even further—from 879 in 1991 to 820 in 2001, which is not a good sign for balancing sex components.

## 2.4 Studies on Female Foeticide

The deficit of females in India's population in past was, thus, attributed mainly to male preponderance at birth, differential in mortality, and underenumeration of females. There was a marked improvement in the quality of data in censuses of 1991 and 2001. There has been an improvement in the mortality of females due to increased availability of health-care facilities, improved literacy and prosperity levels. In view of this, the decline in the sex ratio attracted the attention of demographers and social scientists alike. Now scholars have attributed this to be widespread misuse of medical technology for identification of the sex of the baby in the mother's womb, and subsequent termination of pregnancy, if the baby is female. This practice is known as 'female foeticide'. One of the techniques used for sex identification is amniocentesis.

Kundu and Sahu (1991) in their study, on the basis of 1991 data, argued that a sharp increase in sex ratio at birth in favour of male babies could be due to amniocentesis. This generated a debate among the scholars. Some scholars (e.g. Rajan *et al.*, 1991) contested this explanation initially. But now there is a general unanimity among scholars regarding the role of amniocentesis, or other techniques for sex identification, and female foeticide in recent decline in sex ratio in India's population (Premi and Raju, 1992).

George and Dahiya (1998) in their study of six villages in undivided Rohtak district in Haryana have confirmed the widespread practice of sex selective termination of pregnancy. According to them, the practice is more prevalent among upper caste Hindus than among Scheduled Castes. They argue that transfer of reproductive technology to India is resulting in reinforcement of patriarchal values, as professional medical organizations seem to be indifferent to ethical misconduct.

Hassan (2000), in a study on sex composition of population in Haryana, has examined the main determinants of the recent decline in sex ratio in the state in terms of net migration, mortality experiences of males and females, and changing sex ratio at birth. He has attributed the recent decline in sex ratio in Haryana to widening sex differentials in mortality among children and the incidence of female foeticide. Decline in child sex ratio, despite an improvement in overall sex ratio during 1991 and 2001, occupied the centre state of discussion (Premi, 2001; Kundu, 2001; Bose, 2001; Gosal, 2002). These studies have particularly drawn attention towards a drastic fall in sex ratio in economically well-off states. Prominent among these states are Punjab, Haryana, Gujarat and Maharashtra among others.

Evidences indicate a growing masculinisation of sex ratio at birth during the recent past. It has convincingly been argued by scholars that the growing male preponderance at birth is because of the practice of sex selective abortions in the areas where strong son preference prevails. In this context Bhat and Zavier (2007) have examined the factors affecting the use of prenatal diagnostic techniques and sex ratio at birth in India. Based on both census data as well as NFHS reports of the two rounds, they have concluded that "while income and education are found to increase the use of prenatal diagnostic technique, their misuse is governed more by cultural factors and the sex composition of the children already born." The study shows that the use of prenatal diagnostic techniques, their misuse is governed more by cultural factors and the sex composition of the children already born. One study shows that the use of the technique is much higher in the urban areas among educated women those with high level of standard of living, non-working women and those regularly exposed to media. In areas with strong preference of sons, the effect of the misuse of the technology is quite evident. On the regional patterns in sex ratio at birth, the study discovered that sex ratio at birth is more masculine in the north-western parts of the country than elsewhere.

## 2.5 Studies on Sex-Selective Abortions

The growing menace of sex selective abortion has attracted the attention of researchers. There are laws against the practice but the same goes unabated, almost through the length and breadth of this country. In Haryana, "it is estimated that 43 per cent of the female foetuses are likely to have been aborted" according to a study by Fred Arnold and T.K. Roy entitled 'Sex Ratio and Sex Selective Abortion in India: Findings from the 1998-99 National Family Health Survey' (Bose, 2002).

In a study conducted by Arnold, Kishor and Roy (2001) aimed to present evidence on use of amniocentesis for sex selection of children, found that use of amniocentesis or ultrasound is varying according to sex composition of previous children. Couples with sons are more likely to have sex selective induced abortions. According to the study, there are 1.3 million induced abortions in India every year, of which over 1 lakh are sex selective abortions following an ultrasound/amniocentesis test.

The mean age of women who had underwent a sex selective abortion was 24.8 years. Sex selective abortion seekers were significantly more likely to come from joint families and were of better economic conditions. This may be due to their low autonomy and mobility, and were less likely to play a major role in family decision-making. All the 263 abortions that had taken place were not during the women's first pregnancy but in later stages. Sex selective abortions were preceded by a sex determination test and 97 per cent of them took place in the private clinics (Ganatra, Hirve and Rao, 2001).

Krishnamoorthy (2003) has derived estimates of the number of sex selective abortions in India using the data on number of live births classified by sex drawn from the NFHS-2. He suggests the practice is prevalent in both rural and urban areas although in the latter it is of much higher magnitude. Krishnamoorthy also suggest that the practice is prevalent among women of all levels of education, and it increases with rising levels of education and development.

Perianayagam (2005) presented a paper based on NFHS-I and NFHS-II. The findings reveal that the rise in sex ratio at birth was steeper in the northern region, while the western and eastern regions showed moderate rise. The sex ratio at birth was higher in urban areas compared to rural areas in most of the Indian states. Sex ratio at last birth shows a steep rise in northern and western states and moderate to marginal increase in the remaining states, suggesting that modern technological tests such as sonogram, ultrasound and amniocentesis had been widely used for sex detection and consequent abortion of female foetuses. Study further found that the excess female child mortality was very high at ages 1-4, and was highest in Haryana (134 per cent), followed by Punjab (81 per cent) and Uttar Pradesh (70 per cent) and a very high level of neglecting female children (25-45 per cent shortfall compared to males) was observed in immunization coverage in most of the northern states.

In a study based on a survey of 2,590 households and 2,646 ever married women in Jind district of Haryana, Unisa, Pujari and Usha (2007) have made an attempt to assess the magnitude of sex selective abortions. The study also examined the underlying reasons for the practice in the state. According to the study, there are ample evidences of the practice in sex selective abortions in rural Haryana. The authors suggest that there has been a marked increase in the number of such cases during the last three decades. Around one-fifth of the women surveyed in the study area had abortions, out of which more than one-third had sex selective abortions.

Patel (2010), a sociologist, in her interesting paper entitled "Risky Lives: Indian Girls Caught between Individual Rationality and Public Good", explores the savvy couple that exercises reproductive choice and makes informed about careful reproductive decisions. It being in control of their lives, couples act what is in their best interest. The question this paper is trying to address is how does one understand the logic that individual rational action leads to public good? Patel, based on her extensive fieldwork in northern India, illustrates how changing family and community characteristics influence the gender equations within the family as well as the fertility decision-making of the household. Couples may not be certain of outcomes of raising daughters, but they try to assess some probabilities of taking or averting the risk of having to raise one or more daughters.

In their paper, Larsen *et al.* (2010), entitled "Inter-Generational Interests, Uncertainty and Decimation: Declining Child Sex Ratios in India" deal with the continuing decline in child sex ratios despite improvements in general welfare and of female status in the society and point to deeply rooted structures of gender inequality. This paper builds upon the recognition that the declining child sex ratios are a result of an ongoing societal change. At the centre of the factors concerning, the problem of daughter discrimination stands the family. The problem of *'missing girls'* can be ascribed to social, economic and cultural factors, which together create incentives for son preference and disincentives for raising daughters. However, it is within the family that the decision-making takes place. Hence, it is of importance to analyze the relationships between these factors with a focus on the family. In order to understand why female children are at risk and why there is an increasing discrimination against girls in India, it is particularly important to consider the intra-household allocation of resources. The parents, as a reaction to the uncertainly that those very changes produce, 'fall back' on traditional norms regarding gender and domestic roles. This makes the bargaining situation and the criteria for the allocation of resources highly adversarial for girls, creating a structure in which there is little space for daughters. Looking at areas both in the north and the south of India, which have shown significant decline in the child sex ratios in the last two decades, the paper draws on from recently conducted field studies of the areas of Karnataka in the south and Uttaranchal in the north.

There is an increasing conflict between preferred family size and preferred sex composition of children in many societies undergoing fertility transition. A substantial decline in the fertility presupposes a desire for fewer children and the means to limit the family size. The widespread use of advanced technologies for sex determination and sex-selective abortion has given a new means for parents to achieve the desired gender composition of their children. In communities where son preference co-exists with discrimination against daughters, stronger the son preference, more intense is the daughter discrimination. The paper entitled "From Fertility Control to Gender Control: Evidences of Gender Discrimination in Rural South India" by Sekher *et al.* (2010) attempt to examine whether fertility decline has led to an increased elimination of daughters. This paper, based on two village studies, carried out in low fertility regions of Karnataka and Tamil Nadu states, provides useful insights into the emerging forms of gender discrimination. Through household surveys, interviews and focus group discussions, the study analyzed the changing attitudes of the peasant communities of the district. It was observed that rapid fertility decline, not accompanied by changes in the cultural values and gender inequality, was in a way responsible for a deliberate attempt to get rid of the girls. In other words, the strong son preference, the increasing pressure on limited land, and spiraling cost of marriage and dowry compel the couples to avoid having daughters. The observations from the villages indicate an intensification of gender bias along with drastic decline in fertility and the increasing preference for sons has manifested in a deliberate discrimination towards daughters.

In an interesting paper, Mari Bhat and Francis Zavier (2007) analyse the effect of Prenatal Diagnostic Technique (PNDT) use on the sex ratio at birth. Data from 2001 census reveals that the sex ratio at birth may have increased by 6 percentage points in India since 1985 and in some parts by 20 per cent points. According to their analysis, the effect of PNDT use on the sex ratio at birth is found to be contingent on whether women are in the male-selection situation or not. While income and education are found to increase the use of PNDT, their misuse is more governed by cultural factors and the sex composition of children already born. Although the use of PNDT is now fairly common in many parts of India, only a minority of couples who use these techniques misuse it for aborting female foetuses. The higher sex ratio at birth observed among more educated and higher income groups is mainly because of their better access to these techniques rather than from their greater misuse.

Prakasam (2010) in his paper entitled "Imbalance in Sex Ratio in Rural Tamil Nadu: A Case Study of Salem District" made an attempt to analyse the imbalances in sex ratio in rural areas of Tamil Nadu. Among the districts of Tamil Nadu, Salem district shows very low sex ratio (680 females per 1000 males). Research investigations are made to explore the reasons for this gender disparity in a state otherwise known for its significant progress in socio-economic development. An attempt was made to find out the variation in sex ratio in Salem district and the prevalence of sex-selective abortion contributing to imbalances. To know the prevalence of sex-selective abortion, data were derived from a survey conducted in Salem district during 2003. The survey covers

1,565 currently married women in the age-group 15-49 who have experienced at least one delivery. Reproductive history of the currently married women and the reasons for undergoing repeated abortions have been examined. Besides these, case studies have been conducted to elicit information on the practices of infanticide and foeticide. Qualitative data analysis revealed that female foeticides and infanticides are very much in practice because of the prevalent dowry system and existing poverty in some communities.

The paper on "Traditions in Transformation: Emerging Son Preference Attitudes among the Nairs of Kerala", by Sudha *et al.* (2010) examines the changing gender preferences among the Nair community of Kerala state in southern India—whether preconditions for gender bias (preference for male children) have emerged among this group and whether gender bias is expressed, either verbally or in the uptake of modern reproductive technologies for prenatal sex selection. Kerala has been lauded in the demographic literature for high achievements: 'normal' sex ratios, near total literacy, long life expectancy, low fertility and good health service coverage—all at a low level of economic development. The status of women is considered to be high in Kerala, attributed to the matrilineal kinship system historically practiced by several groups in the state, including the Nairs. However, matrilineal kinship had been dismantled over the previous century; and high female unemployment, dowry custom, domestic violence, and other negative features are widespread in Kerala today. The authors conducted interviews using rapid ethnographic assessment methods among three generations of Nair men and women living in the Thrissur urban area. The results show that patrilineal kinship and family organization, changes in marriage customs, spread of dowry, and gender-based division of labour in the household and at work have penetrated into the Nair community. Verbal expressions of gender bias are widespread. Modern prenatal sex-selection techniques appear to exist on a very small scale and are not in wide evidence as in northern parts of India. This interesting study is a unique contribution to the existing literature of female deficit in India, as it examines a community never before researched from this perspective but which has a cultural background assumed to protect against gender bias.

Improving the status of women, through varied policies and programmes, will automatically improve the status of girls in the family and society, has proved to be ineffective. Even in countries where women enjoy high status, girls are less preferred to boys. There are basically three factors of son preference in India, viz. economic utility, socio-cultural utility and religious functions. The studies indicate that sons are more preferred than daughters to provide labour, earn wages and as old-age support for parents. Upon marriage, a son, in the form of his wife, makes an addition and asset to the family providing assistance in household work and brings an economic reward through dowry payments, while daughters get married of and merit an economic penalty through dowry charges. The socio-cultural utility factor of son preference implies that in India's patriarchal system of families having at least one son is mandatory in order to continue the familial lineage and many sons constitute additional status to families.

The paper, entitled "Status of the Girl Child and Son Preference in Madurai", authored by Mumtaj Begam and Christianna Singh (2010), examines the effect of socio-economic characteristics on the actual probability of having sons through a maximum likelihood logistic estimation in city such as Madurai with its strong traditional bind. Primary data collected through a survey of 300 samples drawn from varied strata is used. Since, the perceived cost of the girl child is higher; the preference for sons is stronger. When the perceived cost of the girls child is reduced, her status is improved and son preference weekened. Awareness is the prime tool to achieve this, and according to authors formulating strategies for empowering girls are the beginning of women's empowerment.

In the context of declining sex ratio, it is important to examine the implications on *'marriage squeeze'* and marriage pattern, which has a serious bearing on quality of life and status of women in India. In demographic literature, *'marriage squeeze'* is understood as imbalance in the sex ratio in the marriageable age-group. When there is increase in the supply of females, it is termed as the female marriage market squeeze and *vice versa*. The study, entitled "Implications of Declining Sex Ratio on Marriage Squeeze of India" by Priyajit Samaiyar and William Joe (2010), examines the marriage squeeze through the measurement methods involving sex ratio and age distribution of marriage. Marriage pattern can be understood as the variables like delayed marriage, age gap between the spouses, and the proportion never married in the population over different marriage cohorts and periods. The analysis carried out using the National Family Health Survey (NFHS), National Sample Survey Organization (NSSO) and census data discusses the socio-economic correlates of marriage squeeze in terms of examining the relationship of marriage squeeze with the selected indicators of marriage pattern. The study demonstrates how the government policy of promoting two-child norm without giving consideration to the problem of sex-selective abortions can actually aggravate the problem of sex imbalance in the country. This declining sex ratio has direct and serious consequences on the marriage market.

Agarwal and Unisa (2010), in their paper entitled "Active and Passive Elimination of Girl Child: Findings from Rural Haryana", highlight the sex-selective discrimination in their terms of active and passive elimination of girl child in different socio-economic conditions as a life course approach. The study has used primary data collected from 329 ever-married women in five villages of Haryana. Active elimination has been seen in terms of abortion according to the sex of the surviving children, pregnancy order, women's childhood experience, autonomy status and marital instability. Autonomy, education and exposure to mass media have negative impact, whereas co-residence with in-laws and no male child have significant positive impact for active elimination. In-laws play an important role in abortion under the umbrella of son preference. In logistic regression results, sex of the children ever born and autonomy were found to be significant factors. The quantitative as well as qualitative data shows that there exists extreme sex-selective discrimination against the girl child in the rural society through conception to their rearing and bearing. Woman, who herself had a worst childhood experience (in terms of discrimination in all spheres including childhood status, food, education, mobility, etc.), had less autonomy in various dimensions, and felt high instability in her married life, is more responsible for the discrimination against girl child leading to a vicious cycle of gender deprivation and discrimination.

The implications of the low sex ratio for future marriages have as yet been little studied in India. It is obvious that less and declining number of girls children as revealed by the 2001 Census will lead to a larger *'bride shortage'* that is already begin experienced in certain northern states of India. The paper, entitled "Across-

Region Marriages: Poverty, Female Migration and Sex Ratio" by Ravinder Kaur, addresses the less explored question of how society deals with this socially and culturally created demographic imbalance. Given that marriage is socially valued and physically/ economically necessary, what is the range of responses and solutions devised by society in order to meet the shortage? Do these solutions (e.g. across-region marriages, polyandry, and forced bachelorhood) differ in different regions and over different time periods? Related to these questions are the implications for society of the excess number of bachelors, the impact of shortage of brides on dowry values, and the changing contours of the marriage market. This sociological study first establishes the parameters of *'bride shortage'* at present and in future in India. Second, based on primary ethnographic research in selected districts of Haryana, U.P. and West Bengal, it explores the strategies adopted by 'needy' men and their families to address the shortage of brides.

In general, the sex ratio can be considered as a direct indicator of women's status and welfare. There have been a number of studies, which have attempted to illustrate how the decline in fertility will affect gender bias and more imbalances in juvenile sex ratios (Clark, 2000; Croll, 2002; Bhat and Zavier, 2003).

However, there is hardly any study, which is concerned, with the balancing population sex components in Haryana. The proposed research project will be a modest attempt to know the attitude of people towards females and various causes responsible for the increasing incidence of female foeticide resulting into missing unborn girls in Haryana, mainly responsible for skewed sex ratio. The present research project has also endeavoured to find out the remedial measures to restore the gender balance in Haryana and thus, has filled up the research gap.

# 3 Conceptual Framework

## 3.1 Sex Ratio

Age and sex composition occupies a very important position in any discussion on characteristics of a population. Age represents a person's potential to work. On the basis of age structure, any population can be classified as young or adult population. Sex is a biological characteristic that classifies human beings into males and females. Sex composition refers to the balance between males and females in the total population. Age and sex composition not only affects the demographic processes, but also determines the socio-economic relationship within a community. Therefore, separate data on males and females and by age becomes a very important tool for various types of planning.

Every population has a unique age and sex composition. The balance between male and female in the total population as well in various age-groups can have considerable impact on social and economic situation in both present and future contexts.

Sex composition is expressed in terms of a ratio between the numerical strength of males and females in total population. Sex composition has significant bearings on fertility levels, life expectancy, mortality conditions, migration and marital status. In other words, sex composition of a population governs the various demographic features in a community. 'As the two sexes play partly contrasting and partly complementary roles in economy and society, the study of the sex composition assumes added significance for a population geographer' (Chandna, 1986).

Sex composition determines the role and status of women, the type of marriages, age at marriage, rate of male and female participation at work, the type and stage of development of economy, etc. According to Momsen (1987), 'Sex ratio, or the number of males per hundred females in a population, would both define the relative quality of life and denote the value placed by society on the sexes'.

The most commonly used measure to represent the sex composition of a population is sex ratio. Sex ratio may be defined as the number of males per 100 or 1000 females or *vice versa*. It may also be expressed as the percentage of total population made up of either males or females. However, ratio is always preferred to percentage, as it is a traditional or conventional tool used in the population studies throughout the world. Sex ratio in the Indian context is defined as the number of females per thousand males in a population. Now-a-days, the term Female-Male Ratio (FMR) is increasingly being used to signify the balance between the two sexes in a population. Here, in the present study, both the terms have been used interchangeably. For example, according to the 2001 census, there were 97,55,331 females and 1,13,27,658 males in Haryana, the sex ratio for the state, thus works out to be 861. In other words, there are 861 females per thousand males in the population of Haryana. The sex ratio can be examined with reference to its three different types, viz. primary sex ratio, secondary sex ratio and tertiary sex ratio. The primary sex ratio refers to ratio between male and female at the time of conception. It is biologically in favour of males. The secondary sex ratio denotes the ratio between two sexes at a time of birth (SRB). Sex ratio at birth in a population is generally in favour of males due to biological reasons. The tertiary sex ratio refers to the ratio of the two sexes in the population at the time of enumeration. In any study on population composition, we are generally concerned with the latter two types of sex ratios. The sex ratio can be calculated for a population as a whole, or for different age groups or for different caste or social groups or for rural and urban areas separately.

### 3.2 Femicide

The practice of *Female Foeticide* has been a centuries-old practice in rural India, so much so that it has become more predominant in the rural parts of India. However, the practice of *femicide,* in which an unborn baby is aborted or killed at birth simply because it is not a boy, is increasingly spreading from India's poor and rural classes to affluent urban families. Selection of the sex of the foetus is a combination of personal choices, family issues, social, ethical, medical and even legal reasons.

The Indian girl child is part of the society, which idolizes sons. This stems from the deep-rooted ancient concept of having a son to carry on with the name and tradition of the family. Right from childhood, girls are made to accept the norms of patriarchal and male dominated society and they thus grow up accepting themselves to be inferior to boys. It is unfortunate that our society considers 'male' as the bread winner for the family, and, therefore, a more valuable asset than a girl child, who is looked upon as a liability in the family. Another key reason for *femicide* has been the system of dowry, prevalent in rural as well as now increasingly in urban India. Since, most of the Indian population is at the poverty level, it is not possible to sustain a girl child because of the prevailing system.

The darker side of the problem arises from the want to get rid of the baby girl by the way of abortion. This follows from abortion been legalized by the Government of India in 1971, leaving no room for debate about the necessity for the same. There can be no argument about the necessity to terminate pregnancy for medical reasons like congenital abnormalities and X-linked disorders. The fact that it has a genesis in the prenatal determination of sex is emphasized by the urban predominance due to availability of such facilities.

Sex Determination Techniques (SDT) which is a Pre-natal Diagnostic Technique (PNDT) is used for predicting the sex of an unborn offspring after conception preferably in the first four months of pregnancy. Such techniques are making inroads in the rural areas, whereby tilting the balance in favour of males by the way of female foeticide.

The problem stands at a very thin dividing line between the medical reasons for termination of pregnancy and female foeticide based on antenatal sex determination. Selective abortions of the female foetuses in the 70s and 80s became common and led to severe disturbances in the male-female ratio over a period of time.

India is one of the few countries where the overall sex ratio has been unfavourable to females. According to population survey reports, the sex ratio which was 972 females per 1000 males in 1901 was 933 females to 1000 males in 2001. The disparity in the ratio was more severe in Delhi, Haryana, Gujarat, Maharashtra, Punjab and Chandigarh. The Child Sex Ratio (CSR) in India has also been indicative of a negative trend towards girl child for decades now. The sharp decline in CSR from 945 in 1991 to 927 in 2001 as brought forth by the 2001 census hit the public eye. Sociologists have speculated that such an imbalance would lead to greater incidence of rape, sharing of women within and outside wedlock, abductions, and in genital, in reducing women's freedom and mobility.

While there exists no quick and easy solution to the problem, it is possible to reduce gender inequality, which lies at the core of *femicide.* The first critical step is to challenge the patriarchal attitudes that applaud boys and undermine girls, and to create a culture that celebrates both the genders equally. More so, the medical fraternity can do a lot of service by preventing the practice of female foeticide.

### 3.3 Sex-Selective Abortion

Sex-selective abortion is the practice of terminating a pregnancy based upon the predicted sex of the foetus. The selective abortion of female fetuses is most common in areas where cultural norms value male children over female children.

Sex-selective abortion was rare before the late 20th century, because of the difficulty of determining the sex of the foetus before birth, but ultrasound has made such selection easier. Prior to this, parents would alter family sex compositions through infanticide.

Sex detection can be performed by the means of one of the two standard genetic tests, CVS and amniocentesis. These may, in principle, be performed as early as the 8th and the 9th week of pregnancy. The difficulty of these tests and the risk of damage to the foetus, potentially resulting in miscarriage or congenital abnormalities (especially when done early during the pregnancy), make them quite uncommon during the first trimester.

Sex selective abortions may be used to avoid birth of children of an undesired sex after the sex of the foetus has been determined.

Female foetuses are aborted after three and half months when the sex of the foetus becomes recognized. During the last few years, cases of abortion have raised significantly and people of rural areas are flocking in large numbers for induced abortions. The cost of abortion ranges from Rs. 2000 to Rs. 5000 depending upon the client's status as well as the status of the nursing home.

Couples with one or two daughters mostly go for abortions, as they don't want additional daughters. Abortion is rarely resorted to in respect with the first child and the birth of the daughter is tolerated also. There is a pressure for abortion by the neighbours and friends who advise the couple for resorting to abortion. This has become an accepted practice among the people.

The selective abortion of female foetuses is most common in areas where cultural norms value male children over female children. A son is often preferred as an 'asset' since he can earn and support the family; a daughter is a 'liability' since she will be married off to another family, and so will not contribute financially to her parents. The patriarchal structure of a society is the single most important factor skewing the sex ratio in favour of males, accentuated in some cultures by the burden of raising a dowry for a daughter's marriage. Openness to the very concept of sex selection is a significant factor: among societies which practice selective female abortion now-a-days, many were systematically practicing female infanticide (either directly or by withholding post-natal care from children of undesirable sex) long before abortion became a viable option.

Some of the respondents openly admitted that they are in favour of abortion of female foetuses because it is very difficult to get their daughters married to a suitable boy. They consider them a liability. They said that today, educating a girl is also essential to find a suitable match for her. This brings dual burden on the family, one for education and the other for dowry, which is the major cause for female foeticide.

Sex-selective abortion has been seen as worsening the sex ratio in India, affecting gender issues related to sex compositions of Indian households. According to the decennial Indian census, the sex ratio in the 0-6 age-group in India went from 104 males per 100 females in 1981, to 105.8 in 1991, to 107.8 in 2001, to 109.4 in 2011. The ratio is significantly higher in certain states such as Punjab and Haryana (126.1 and 122.0, as of 2001). The use of ultrasound and abortion for sex selection has been banned since 1994 in India. However, there is evidence that such bans are rarely enforced and numerous dedicated sex selection clinics operate in many regions of those countries. The practice is most common among educated and wealthy residents, who are most likely to afford the procedure. In an article published in *The Lancet*, Indian census data was analyzed and concluded that selective abortion of female foetuses has increased in India over the past few decades due to increased prenatal sex determination and has contributed to a widening imbalance in the child sex ratio, though the basis of the finding has been questioned.

A 2005 study estimated that over 90 million females were "missing" from the expected population in Afghanistan, Bangladesh, China, India, Pakistan, South Korea and Taiwan alone, and suggested that sex-selective abortion plays a role in this deficit. India's 2011 census shows a serious decline in the number of girls under the age of seven—activists fear eight million female foetuses may have been aborted between 2001 and 2011. Some research suggests that culture plays a larger role than economic conditions in gender preference and sex-selective abortion. Other demographers, however, argue that perceived gender imbalances may arise from the underreporting of female births, rather than sex-selective abortion or infanticide.

Sex-selective abortion was rare before the late 20th century, because of the difficulty of determining the sex of the foetus before birth, but ultrasound has made such selection easier. Prior to this, parents would alter family sex compositions through infanticide.

The Prenatal Diagnostic and Prevention Act, 1994, has been violated because the increased accessibility has made it possible for villagers to reach at such diagnostic centres located in nearby towns.

# 4 Socio-Economic and Demographic Characteristics of the Population Surveyed

## 4.1 Household Characteristics

### *4.1.1 Household Composition*

Out of the total of 56,934 households from target villages, the sampled households (20 per cent) comprises of 11,357 in number. On an average, households in Haryana are comprised of 5.7 persons per household. The urban size of household is 5.2 persons, whereas in rural Haryana, this size is 5.9 persons per household. But in case of study area, the average size of household is smaller (5.0 persons per household) than the state as a whole (5.7 persons per household) (Table 4.1).

With regard to household type, 55.7 per cent of the households in Haryana are of the *nuclear type.* The nuclear type of households in urban Haryana is 59.8 per cent, whereas, in rural areas of the

**Table 4.1:** Haryana: Size of Household

| *State/Target Villages* | *No. of Households* | *Population* | *Size of Household (Persons per Household)* |
|---|---|---|---|
| **Haryana** | **37,12,319** | **2,11,44,564** | **5.7** |
| Urban Haryana | 11,70,339 | 61,15,304 | 5.2 |
| Rural Haryana | 25,41,980 | 1,50,29,260 | 5.9 |
| Target Villages | 11,357 | 57,031 | 5.0 |

*Sources:* NFHS-3 and Field Survey.

state, this figure is 53.9 per cent. In the present study, the nuclear household comprises of 58.06 per cent and joint family system is prevalent among 41.94 per cent households (Table 4.2). It means the trend of joint family system is on the way of decline in the modern age of globalization.

**Table 4.2:** Haryana: Household Type

| *State/Target Villages* | *Household Type* | | | |
|---|---|---|---|---|
| | *Nuclear* | | *Joint* | |
| | *Number* | *Per cent* | *Number* | *Per cent* |
| Haryana | 20,67,762 | 55.7 | 16,44,557 | 44.3 |
| Urban Haryana | 6,99,863 | 59.8 | 4,70,476 | 40.2 |
| Rural Haryana | 13,70,127 | 53.9 | 11,71,852 | 46.1 |
| Target Villages | 6,594 | 58.06 | 4,763 | 41.94 |

*Sources:* NFHS-3 and Field Survey.

Table 4.3 shows that 93 per cent of households in Haryana are male-headed households and only seven per cent constituting female-headed households. Eleven per cent of households are headed by women, with 9 per cent of the population living in female-headed households (NFHS-3, Haryana State Report, 2008, p. 2). in the present study, 87.3 per cent head of the households are male. Only 12.7 per cent females are the head of the households, because most of them were widows. This shows that in Haryana, the households are predominantly dominated by males.

**Table 4.3:** Haryana: Head of the Household by Sex

| *State/Target Villages* | *Head of the Household* | | | |
|---|---|---|---|---|
| | *Male* | | *Female* | |
| | *Number* | *Per cent* | *Number* | *Per cent* |
| Haryana | 18,797,517 | 88.9 | 23,47,047 | 11.1 |
| Urban Haryana | 5,454,851 | 89.2 | 6,60,453 | 10.8 |
| Rural Haryana | 13,330,954 | 88.7 | 16,98,306 | 11.3 |
| Target Villages | 9,915 | 87.3 | 1,442 | 12.7 |

*Sources:* NFHS-3 and Field Survey.

The median age of the head of the household in Haryana is 42 years having very little variation. Household heads seem to be somewhat more concentrated in 30-44 age-group in the state.

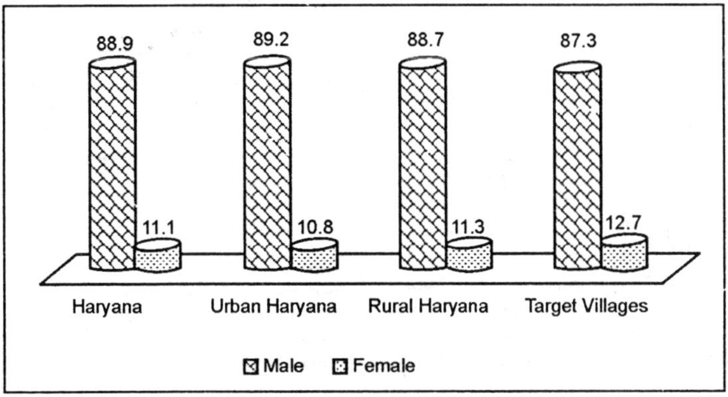


**Fig. 4.1:** Haryana: Head of the Household by Sex.

According to NFHS-3, overall 88.3 per cent of the household heads in Haryana are Hindus and only 6.4 per cent are Muslims. Less than one per cent of the head of the household belong to other religion. Similar is depicted in the field survey where 87.9 per cent household heads are Hindu and 9.1 per cent belong to Muslim community. 2.7 per cent are Sikh and only 0.3 per cent belongs to other religion (Table 4.4).

**Table 4.4:** Haryana: Head of the Household by Religion

| *State/Target Villages* | *Religion of Household Head (Per cent)* | | | |
|---|---|---|---|---|
| | *Hindu* | *Muslim* | *Sikh* | *Others* |
| Haryana | 88.3 | 6.4 | 5.0 | 0.2 |
| Urban Haryana | 94.5 | 2.5 | 2.5 | 0.5 |
| Rural Haryana | 85.5 | 8.2 | 6.2 | 0.1 |
| Target Villages | 87.9 | 9.1 | 2.7 | 0.3 |

*Sources:* NFHS-3 and Field Survey.

### 4.1.2 Housing Characteristics

The majority of households in Haryana (61.1 per cent) live in *pucca* houses. However, the proportion of *pucca* houses in rural areas is

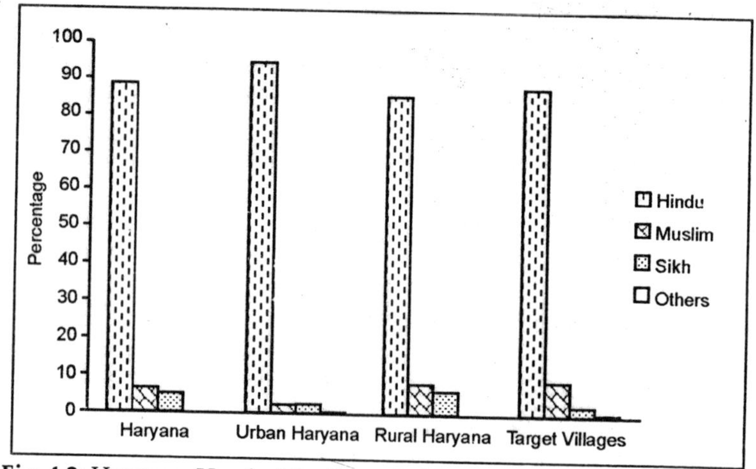


**Fig. 4.2:** Haryana: Head of the Household by Religion.

**Table 4.5:** Haryana: Caste Structure of Households

| *State/Target Villages* | *Caste Structure of Households (%)* | | |
|---|---|---|---|
| | *General* | *Scheduled Castes* | *Backward Castes* |
| Haryana | 52.1 | 24.6 | 22.9 |
| Urban Haryana | 56.6 | 19.2 | 23.9 |
| Rural Haryana | 50.1 | 27.0 | 22.5 |
| Target Villages | 60.9 | 16.9 | 22.2 |

*Sources:* NFHS-3 and Field Survey.

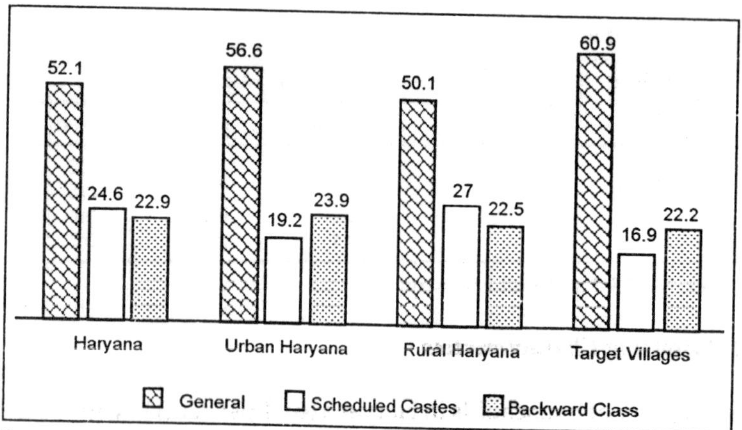


**Fig. 4.3:** Haryana: Caste Structure of Households.

48.5 per cent. Forty-six per cent of the houses in rural areas are *semi-pucca* and only 5.1 per cent are *kachcha* houses (Table 4.6). In case of present study, there was hardly any *kachcha* house inhabited by respondents selected from the target villages. Overall, the condition of more than 50 per cent sampled houses was good.

**Table 4.6:** Haryana: Type of Houses by Rural-Urban Residence

| *Type of House* | *Urban* | *Rural* | *Total* |
|---|---|---|---|
| Kachcha | 0.2 | 5.1 | 3.5 |
| Semi-pucca | 11.1 | 46.4 | 35.3 |
| Pucca | 88.6 | 48.5 | 61.1 |
| Missing | 0.2 | 0 | 0 |
| **Total** | **100** | **100** | **100** |

*Source:* NFHS-3, Haryana State Report, 2008.

Ninety-two per cent of households have electricity, whereas 89 per cent of rural households are characterized by this facility. A little less than two-thirds of rural households (65 per cent) have no toilet facilities, as against only 11 per cent among urban households. Ninety-four per cent of rural households use an improved source of drinking water (NFHS-3, Haryana State Report, 2008).

However, the present study reveals that 94 per cent households in rural Haryana have electricity. With regard to water sources for drinking water, 95.4 per cent of the total households use drinking water from improved sources (30 per cent of households use piped water into dwelling/yard/plot, 28.3 per cent use public tap, 37.1 per cent use hand pump, bore-well and well) and 4.6 per cent use from non-improved sources (Table 4.7).

As far as sanitation facility is concerned, 62 per cent of the households in rural Haryana have no toilet facility. 27.7 per cent households in Haryana have their own toilets with flush facility. The percentage of households using public toilets with flush facility is less than one per cent in rural areas.

Regarding type of fuel used, fire wood is the dominating fuel used by 37.1 per cent people of rural Haryana. It is followed by cow-dung cakes (28.4 per cent), LPG (22.4 per cent), Agricultural crop waste (11.8 per cent) and others (0.3 per cent) (Table 4.8 and Fig. 4.4).

**Table 4.7:** Haryana: Households by Type of Amenities

| *Amenity* | *Per cent of Total Households* | | |
|---|---|---|---|
| | *Urban* | *Rural* | *Total* |
| Households with availability of electricity | 82.9 | 78.5 | 92.9 |
| NFHS | 97.5 | 88.7 | 91.5 |
| **Source of drinking water** | | | |
| Improved source | 98.6 | 94.2 | 95.6 |
| Piped water into dwelling/yard/plot | 62.1 | 29.7 | 39.9 |
| Public tap/standpipe | 8.9 | 27 | 21.3 |
| Tube-well or bore-well | 27.6 | 36.9 | 34 |
| Other improved source | 0.0 | 0.7 | 0.5 |
| Non-improved source | 1.4 | 5.8 | 4.4 |
| **Sanitation facility** | | | |
| **Improved, not shared** | 66.1 | 28.1 | 40 |
| Flush/pour flush to piped sewer system, septic tank, or pit latrine | 65.1 | 25.2 | 37.7 |
| Pit latrine with slab | 1.1 | 2.9 | 2.3 |
| **Not improved** | 33.7 | 71.9 | 59.9 |
| Any facility shared with other households | 21.7 | 6.3 | 11.1 |
| Flush/pour flush not to sewer system, septic tank, or pit latrine | 1.1 | 0.1 | 0.4 |
| Pit latrine without slab/open pit | 0.2 | 1 | 0.8 |
| No facility/open space/field | 10.8 | 64.5 | 47.6 |
| Other | 0.0 | 0.1 | 0 |
| Missing | 0.2 | 0 | 0 |

*Source:* NFHS-3, Haryana State Report, 2008.

**Table 4.8:** Haryana: Households by Type of Fuel Used for Cooking in Rural Areas

| *Cooking Fuel* | *Per cent of Total Households* | |
|---|---|---|
| | *Target Villages* | *NFHS-3* |
| Fire Wood | 37.1 | 39.5 |
| Cow-dung cakes | 28.4 | 29.9 |
| LPG | 22.4 | 10.2 |
| Agricultural crop waste | 11.8 | 13.4 |
| Others | 0.3 | 0.4 |

*Source:* Field Survey and NFHS-3, Haryana State Report, 2008.

### *4.1.3 Households Owning Selected Durable Goods*

It is said that the possession of consumer durable goods is an important indicator of a household's economic status. Table 4.9 shows the percentage distribution of households owning selected durable goods. It is observed from Table 4.9 that in the state of

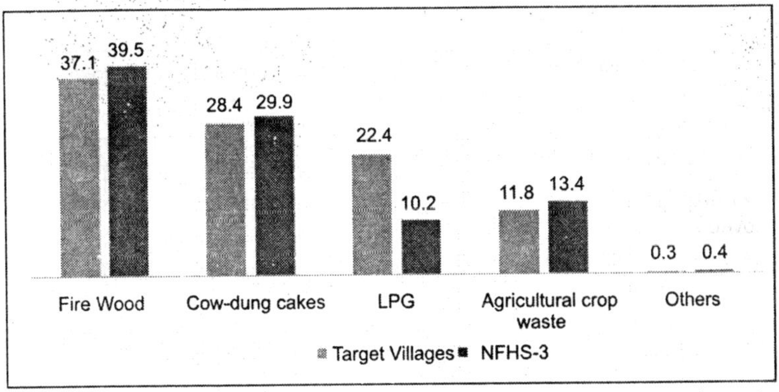


**Fig. 4.4:** Haryana: Households by Type of Fuel used for Cooking in Rural Areas.

**Table 4.9:** Haryana: Households Owning Selected Durable Goods in Rural Areas

| *Household Goods* | *Per cent of Total Households* | |
|---|---|---|
| | *Target Villages* | *NFHS-3 (Rural)* |
| Mattress | 75.8 | 46.8 |
| Pressure cooker | 80.7 | 46.0 |
| Chair | 77.4 | 55.9 |
| Cot or bed | 96.1 | 95.5 |
| Table | 77.5 | 56.3 |
| Electric fan | 93.8 | 82.8 |
| Radio or transistor | 35.6 | 27.3 |
| Television (black and white) | 27.1 | 32.7 |
| Television (colour) | 57.3 | 25.7 |
| Any television | 80.3 | 55.6 |
| Sewing machine | 61.8 | 49.3 |
| Mobile telephone | 41.0 | 15.9 |
| Any other type of telephone | 30.4 | 15.5 |
| Computer | 5.9 | 0.3 |
| Refrigerator | 55.7 | 26.7 |
| Watch or clock | 95.8 | 88.5 |
| Water pump | 10.8 | 8.3 |
| Thresher | 0.3 | 2.0 |
| Tractor | 0.8 | 7.2 |
| Others | 0.0 | 0.5 |

*Source:* Field Survey and NFHS-3, Haryana State Report, 2008.

Haryana, as a whole, majority of the households have cot/bed, electric fan, clock watch, mattress (98.2 per cent, 88.0 per cent, 86.9 per cent and 60 per cent respectively).

Other consumer durable goods often found in most of the households are black and white television (45 per cent), bicycle (42 per cent), chair (45.5 per cent), radio/transistor (31.2 per cent), pressure cooker (28.3 per cent), water pump (20 per cent), scooter/motor-cycle/tractor (10 per cent), telephone (9.5 per cent) and thresher (7 per cent).

### 4.1.4 Occupational Structure of the Respondents

In Haryana, majority of people are engaged in primary activities especially agricultural activities, because Haryana is well-known agricultural state, major share of its economy comes from agriculture only. Now-a-days, industrialization in Haryana is increasing rapidly, yet it is basically an agricultural state. Same is depicted in our sample which shows that 69.2 per cent respondents were engaged in agricultural activities, only 9.0 per cent are engaged in secondary activities and 21.7 per cent are involved in tertiary activities (Table 4.10 and Fig. 4.5).

**Table 4.10:** Haryana: Occupational Structure of Respondents

| *Occupational Structure* | *No. of Households* | *Percentage* |
|---|---|---|
| Primary | 7859 | 69.2 |
| Secondary | 1022 | 9.0 |
| Tertiary | 2465 | 21.7 |
| Quaternary | 11 | 0.1 |

*Source:* Field Survey.

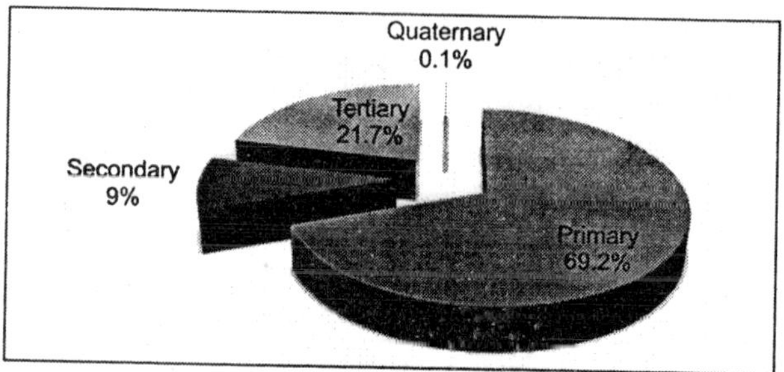


**Fig. 4.5:** Haryana: Occupational Structure of Respondents.

## 4.2 Age and Sex Composition

As revealed by Haryana State Report of NFHS-3, thirty-five per cent of Haryana's population is under age 15; only 5 per cent is age 65 and above. However, the present study reveals that 28.28 per cent of the population in Haryana is below 15 years of age, 50.3 per cent population is in age-group 15-44 and only 8.48 per cent are aged 60 or more (Table 4.11).

**Table 4.11:** Haryana: Household Population by Age and Sex

| *Age Group* | *Household Population* | | | | |
|---|---|---|---|---|---|
| | *Male* | *Female* | *Total* | *Per cent to Total* | *Sex Ratio* |
| 0-4 | 2,123 | 1,523 | 3,646 | 6.39 | 717 |
| 5-9 | 3,581 | 2,486 | 6,067 | 10.64 | 694 |
| 10-14 | 3,721 | 2,696 | 6,417 | 11.25 | 725 |
| 15-19 | 3,625 | 2,772 | 6,397 | 11.22 | 765 |
| 20-24 | 2,969 | 2,435 | 5,404 | 9.48 | 820 |
| 25-29 | 2,620 | 2,274 | 4,894 | 8.58 | 868 |
| 30-34 | 2,224 | 2,022 | 4,246 | 7.45 | 909 |
| 35-39 | 2,159 | 1,946 | 4,105 | 7.20 | 901 |
| 40-44 | 1,966 | 1,663 | 3,629 | 6.36 | 846 |
| 45-49 | 1,786 | 1,509 | 3,295 | 5.78 | 845 |
| 50-54 | 1,371 | 1,088 | 2,459 | 4.31 | 794 |
| 55-59 | 925 | 706 | 1,631 | 2.86 | 763 |
| 60-64 | 937 | 785 | 1,722 | 3.02 | 838 |
| 65-69 | 702 | 565 | 1,267 | 2.22 | 805 |
| 70-74 | 562 | 378 | 940 | 1.65 | 673 |
| 75-79 | 247 | 163 | 410 | 0.72 | 660 |
| 80+ | 315 | 187 | 502 | 0.87 | 594 |
| **Total** | **31,833** | **25,198** | **57,031** | **100.0** | **792** |

*Source*: Field Survey.

## 4.3 Literacy and Educational Attainment

In NFHS-3, literate persons are those who have either completed at least standard six or passed a simple literacy test conducted as a part of the survey. According to this measure, 60 per cent of women (age 15-49) and 83 per cent of men (age 15-49) are literate.

Thirty-eight per cent of women and 14 per cent of men (age 15-49) have never been to school. Forty-four per cent of men have completed 10 or more years of education, but only 30 per cent of women have attained that level of education. (NFHS-3 Haryana State Report, 2008)

**Table 4.12:** Haryana: Tehsil-wise Rural Literacy Rates by Sex, 2001

| *District* | *State/Tehsils* | *Rural Literacy Rate (Per cent)* | | |
|---|---|---|---|---|
| | | *Total* | *Male* | *Female* |
| | **Haryana** | **63.19** | **75.37** | **49.26** |
| Panchkula* | Kalka | 63.22 | 72.29 | 52.64 |
| | Panchkula | 67.97 | 76.70 | 56.54 |
| Ambala | Naraingarh | 66.40 | 75.24 | 56.45 |
| | Ambala | 70.23 | 78.41 | 61.08 |
| | Barara | 72.38 | 80.82 | 63.15 |
| Yamunanagar | Jagadhri | 67.23 | 75.91 | 57.34 |
| | Chhachhrauli | 58.40 | 67.58 | 47.83 |
| Kurukshetra | Shahbad | 69.69 | 78.47 | 49.93 |
| | Pehowa | 60.34 | 69.36 | 50.29 |
| | Thanesar | 67.10 | 76.39 | 56.61 |
| Kaithal | Guhla | 54.75 | 63.46 | 45.03 |
| | Kaithal | 56.04 | 67.37 | 42.79 |
| Karnal | Nilokheri | 64.38 | 73.92 | 53.56 |
| | Indri | 66.85 | 76.43 | 56.02 |
| | Karnal | 63.31 | 72.78 | 52.41 |
| | Assandh | 60.37 | 69.77 | 59.74 |
| | Gharaunda | 61 42 | 72.66 | 48.49 |
| Panipat | Panipat | 64.81 | 75.78 | 51.65 |
| | Israna | 65.23 | 77.62 | 50.90 |
| | Samalkha | 63.04 | 74.83 | 48.98 |
| Sonipat | Gohana | 67.89 | 79.55 | 54.38 |
| | Ganaur | 67.83 | 80.00 | 53.49 |
| | Sonipat | 73.19 | 84.30 | 59.82 |
| | Kharkhoda | 68.67 | 79.45 | 55.79 |
| Jind | Narwana | 52.86 | 65.46 | 38.28 |
| | Jind | 60.94 | 73.91 | 45.57 |
| | Julana | 65.38 | 78.23 | 50.43 |
| | Safidon | 62.47 | 73.92 | 49.07 |
| Fatehabad | Ratia | 49.77 | 58.38 | 40.37 |
| | Tohana | 53.95 | 64.19 | 42.46 |
| | Fatehabad | 56.58 | 68.86 | 42.79 |
| Sirsa | Dabwali | 54.16 | 73.87 | 43.38 |
| | Sirsa | 56.37 | 67.16 | 44.29 |
| | Rania | 57.97 | 68.43 | 46.23 |
| | Ellenabad | 53.09 | 63.96 | 41.10 |
| Hisar | Adampur | 60.87 | 75.01 | 44.79 |
| | Hisar | 60.07 | 73.25 | 44.56 |
| | Narnaund | 58.58 | 71.96 | 43.00 |
| | Hansi | 60.68 | 74.12 | 45.01 |
| Bhiwani | Bawani Khera | 62.84 | 75.89 | 48.06 |
| | Bhiwani | 65.55 | 78.00 | 51.31 |
| | Tosham | 61.65 | 76.10 | 45.24 |
| | Siwani | 60.31 | 75.18 | 43.81 |
| | Loharu | 63.68 | 79.37 | 43.43 |
| | Dadri | 68.22 | 82.38 | 42.57 |

(*Contd.*)

**Table 4.12** (*Contd.*)

| *District* | *State/Tehsils* | *Rural Literacy Rate (Per cent)* | *District* | *State/Tehsils* |
|---|---|---|---|---|
| Rohtak | Maham | 66.66 | 78.60 | 52.50 |
| | Rohtak | 70.58 | 81.97 | 57.09 |
| Jhajjar | Beri | 71.56 | 84.13 | 57.25 |
| | Bahadurgarh | 72.29 | 83.00 | 59.46 |
| | Jhajjar | 68.68 | 80.87 | 54.80 |
| Mahendragarh | Mahendragarh | 69.73 | 84.24 | 54.26 |
| | Narnaul | 67.61 | 83.91 | 50.47 |
| Rewari | Kosli | 74.26 | 88.60 | 59.45 |
| | Rewari | 74.68 | 88.76 | 59.41 |
| | Bawal | 68.78 | 84.41 | 51.74 |
| Gurgaon | Pataudi | 74.45 | 87.73 | 60.11 |
| | Gurgaon | 77.28 | 87.63 | 64.89 |
| | Sohna | 69.61 | 83.35 | 53.98 |
| | Taoru | 53.57 | 70.49 | 34.47 |
| | Nuh | 43.62 | 61.80 | 23.23 |
| | Ferozepur Jhirka | 38.05 | 56.74 | 17.45 |
| | Punahana | 35.33 | 53.65 | 15.26 |
| Faridabad | Faridabad | 62.05 | 76.24 | 45.86 |
| | Ballabgarh | 65.35 | 79.96 | 48.25 |
| | Palwal | 61.79 | 79.00 | 41.73 |
| | Hathin | 44.05 | 61.71 | 43.75 |
| | Hodal | 75.34 | 75.02 | 36.62 |

*Source:* Computed from, Census of India (2001), *Primary Census Abstract*, Haryana, Series 7, Tables A5-A8, Directorate of Census Operations, Haryana.

It is revealed from the Table 4.12 that the highest literacy rate is found in the tehsil of Gurgaon (77.28 per cent), whereas, the lowest literacy rate is in Punahana tehsil (35.33 per cent). In terms of male and female literacy rate, the tehsils of Rewari (88.76 per cent) and Gurgaon (64.89 per cent) are attributed with highest literacy rates respectively. On the other hand, Punahana tehsil is having the lowest literacy rate in terms of male (53.65 per cent) and female (15.26 per cent).

Table 4.13 shows that in Haryana, the total literacy rate of the sampled population is 60.75 per cent in comparison to rural Haryana where total literacy rate is 63.19 per cent. In case of male literacy, sampled population is lagging behind with 66.91 per cent when compared with rural male (75.37 per cent) of Haryana. But female literacy of sampled population is more (53.25 per cent) than the average of rural female literates (49.26 per cent) of Haryana. It shows impact of awareness among women regarding education and the facilities provided to them by government in the form of free education up to graduation level as well as various incentives given to them in rural areas.

**Table 4.13:** Haryana: Level of Education by Sex

| *Level of Education* | *Per cent Literates* | | |
|---|---|---|---|
| | *Total* | *Male* | *Female* |
| Illiterate | 39.25 | 33.09 | 46.75 |
| Primary | 15.57 | 15.56 | 15.58 |
| Middle | 13.14 | 13.44 | 12.77 |
| High | 17.19 | 19.87 | 13.93 |
| Secondary | 8.92 | 10.83 | 6.61 |
| Graduation | 4.22 | 5.16 | 3.07 |
| Post-Graduation | 0.99 | 1.22 | 0.71 |
| Technical (Degree/Diploma) | 0.72 | 0.83 | 0.58 |
| **Total** | **60.75** | **66.91** | **53.25** |

*Source:* Field Survey.

Table 4.13 shows that 39.25 per cent of the population is illiterate in the population of sample survey. 46.75 per cent females and only 33.09 per cent males are illiterate indicating a wide gender disparity in literacy (Fig. 4.6).

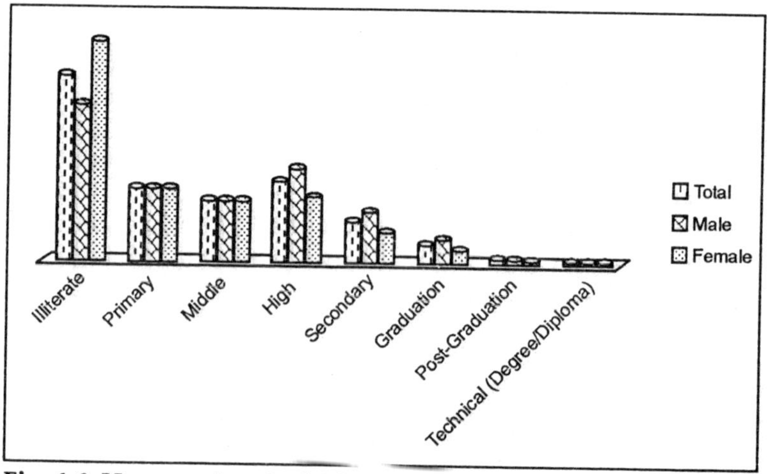


**Fig. 4.6:** Haryana: Level of Education by Sex.

## 4.4 Marital Status

Table 4.14 shows the marital status of the household population according to age and sex for the state of Haryana. In Haryana, among females, 60 per cent are currently married and 34 per cent are never married. The percentage of never married is higher among males (48.2 per cent) than for females in Haryana.

As far as **marital status** is concerned, 97.1 per cent women in Haryana reported to be **currently married** and 2.9 per cent women are **widowed.** The percentage of women who reported to be **divorced/separated** is 4 per cent each. Two to three per cent women said that they were **widows.** Nearly ninety per cent of the respondents reported to be living with their husbands in Haryana. A very small percentage of women were not living with their husbands in the state.

**Table 4.14:** Haryana: Marital Status of the Household Population by Sex

| *Marital Status* | *Per cent Population* | | |
|---|---|---|---|
| | *Total* | *Male* | *Female* |
| Unmarried | 42.42 | 48.83 | 34.32 |
| Currently-married | 53.81 | 48.20 | 60.90 |
| Widowed | 3.76 | 2.96 | 4.78 |
| Separated/Deserted | 0.01 | 0.01 | 0.0 |
| Divorced | 0.0 | 0.0 | 0.0 |
| Never Married | 0.0 | 0.0 | 0.0 |

*Source:* Field Survey.

It is revealed from the Table 4.14 that the percentage of separated/deserted/windowed and divorced is negligible in the sample villages for both the sex. A total of 42.42 per cent and 48.83 per cent male along with 34.32 per cent female are unmarried in the sample households. The percentage of currently married population is 53.81 per cent. Among these 48.20 per cent male and 60.90 per cent female are married.

# 5 Perception and Awareness among Respondents

## 5.1 Need of Education for Boys and Girls

As far as the need of education for boys and girls is concerned in modern society, it has become an essential part of life to sustain. To educate a female is more important because she has to play dual role in society, i.e. one at home and other at workplace. So investment in children's education is an important factor for bringing about transformation in the society. Education makes a person aware of the surroundings about do's and don'ts. In the present study, we find that people in our patriarchal society still consider that girl's education is not as important as that of boys. Table 5.1 provides information on people's perception regarding the need of education for their children.

**Table 5.1:** Haryana: Need of Education for Boys and Girls

| *Perceived Level of Education* | *Percentage of Respondents* | |
|---|---|---|
| | *Boys* | *Girls* |
| No Education | 0.0 | 0.0 |
| Primary | 0.3 | 0.2 |
| Middle | 0.5 | 5.2 |
| High | 5.5 | 20.4 |
| Senior Secondary | 11.2 | 16.7 |
| Graduation | 18.1 | 12.2 |
| Post-graduation | 9.7 | 7.8 |
| As much as He/She Desires | 53.7 | 36.5 |
| Depends on the Economic Condition | 1.0 | 1.0 |

*Source*: Field Survey.

It is revealed from the Table 5.1 that 53.7 per cent respondents believe that boys should be given as much education as they desire followed by graduation level (18.1 per cent), senior secondary (11.2 per cent), post-graduation (9.7 per cent), high school (5.5 per cent) level of education. On the contrary, only 36.5 per cent of respondents believe that a girl should be given as much education as she desires followed by high school (20.4 per cent), senior secondary (16.7 per cent), graduation (12.2 per cent), post-graduation (7.8 per cent), middle school (5.2 per cent) level of education. A very noticeable feature is that in Haryana, all the respondents believe that some education must be imparted to both boys and girls.

## 5.2 Perception about Minimum Age of Marriage for Boys and Girls

It is surprising to see that even after becoming one of the richest states of India (i.e. Haryana), a large number of respondents believe that boys and girls should be married at the age of 21 and 18 respectively (Table 5.2). Among the respondents, 56.9 per cent believe that girls should be married at the age of 18. In comparison 55.8 per cent respondents feel that boys should be married above 21 years of age.

**Table 5.2:** Haryana: Perception about Minimum Age of Marriage for Boys and Girls

| Perceived Age at Marriage | Percentage of Respondents | Perceived Age at Marriage | Percentage of Respondents |
|---|---|---|---|
| | Boys | | Girls |
| Below 21 | 19.7 | Below 18 | 24.4 |
| At 21 | 24.5 | At 18 | 56.9 |
| Above 21 | 55.8 | Above 18 | 18.7 |

*Source*: Field Survey.

**Observations**

1. An old person of village 'Kharhar' said that I had five grandsons, I will marry them immediately after attaining the age of 21 as I know that there is a shortage of girls in Haryana.
2. According to another observation, one respondent told that they are willing to marry their daughter on attaining the age of 18 years because it

*(Contd.)*

becomes unsafe to send her outside the home for studies.

3. It is also observed that people are willing to marry their daughters after secondary education so that they will not have to spend too much on their education which is costlier now-a-days. With that money they prefer to marry the girl as it becomes difficult to get a suitable match if girl is highly qualified. Moreover, a highly qualified groom will demand more dowry.

## 5.3 Age at First Marriage

According to NFHS-3, the median age at first marriage is 17.5 years among women (age 20-49 years) and 21.8 years among men (age 25-49 years). On an average, men get married almost five years later than women.

Forty-one per cent of women (age 20-24 years) got married before the legal minimum age of 18. One-third (34 per cent) of men (age 25-29) years got married before the legal minimum age of 21. But in our sample no one among the respondents revealed that they married their children before attaining the legal age of 18 years and 21 years for their daughters and sons respectively.

**Observations**

1. One '*anganwadi*' worker told that many of the boys and girls are being married before attaining the legal age of marriage. This is a common practice in village but people do not complain against this because of harassments in legal processes. Moreover, this creates rivalry among their families.
2. According to another observation, we find that neither the girl nor her mother was prepared for marriage of the girl before attaining legal age of marriage, i.e. 18 years. Mother told that I and my daughter are forced to do this because my husband is not ready to send her outside the village for education after 10th class.

## 5.4 Fertility Levels

As per NFHS-3, Haryana State Report (2008), at current fertility levels, a woman in Haryana will have an average of 2.7 children in her lifetime, the same as the national fertility level. Fertility decreased by more than one child between NFHS-1 and NFHS-2, but it decreased by only 0.2 children between NFHS-2 and NFHS-3.

Fertility in rural areas is 2.9 children per woman. However, fertility rates are somewhat higher for women in disadvantaged groups (2.9 children per woman among Scheduled Caste women and 3.0 children per woman among Other Backward Classes) than for women who do not belong to Scheduled Castes. In nutshell, fertility in Haryana is at the same level as fertility in India as a whole (2.7 children per woman).

## 5.5 Teenage Pregnancy

Among young women age 15-19 in Haryana, 12 per cent have already begun childbearing, which is 4 percentage points lower than the national average. None of the women age 15 have started childbearing, but by age 19, almost two-fifths (39 per cent) of women have either already had a live birth or are pregnant with their first child. Young women in rural areas are four times as likely to be mothers as young women in urban areas. These statistics reflect the fact that most women in Haryana (particularly in rural areas) marry during their teens. (NFHS-3 Haryana State Report, 2008)

**Observation**

It is experienced during Field Survey that people are aware of legal age of marriage for boys and girls. They are reluctant enough to marry their children before the legal age of marriage whenever they find a suitable match. But they directly do not accept this truth. This in turn, increases teenage pregnancy and increasing incidence of foetal as well as maternal mortality rates.

## 5.6 Infant and Child Mortality

The infant mortality rate in Haryana in NFHS-3 is estimated at 42 deaths before the age of one year per 1,000 live births, down from the NFHS-2 estimate of 57 and the NFHS-1 estimate of 73. However, 1 in 24 children still die within the first year of life, and 1 in 19 die before reaching age five. As expected, boys have a higher mortality rate than girls during the neonatal period (in the first month of life). During the post-neonatal period (ages 1-11 months), the mortality rate is almost the same for girls and boys, but between ages 1 and 5 years, girls are twice as likely to die as boys. Children born to mothers under age 20 and age 30-39 are more likely to die during infancy than children born to mothers in the prime childbearing ages (20-29 years). Infant mortality is 62 per 1,000 live births for teenage mothers and mothers age 30-39, compared with 36 for mothers age 20-29. Infant mortality rates are also higher for Muslims than for Hindus and are higher for Scheduled Castes and Other Backward Classes than for other castes. The infant mortality rate is much higher in rural areas than in urban areas. The infant mortality rate is also much higher for children whose mothers have no education (46 per 1,000) than for children whose mothers have completed 10 or more years of schooling.

**Observation**

An old woman of 80 said that: "chori chari to nuyen pal jayan karen"

"a girl can survive without too much of efforts, she can even survive the pre-mature delivery of 7 months but if a boy is born pre-mature he will not be able to survive. Biologically girls are stronger than boys. So boys need more care and nutrition that is why, I do take care about my sons and grandsons more than my grand-daughters".

## 5.7 Perceptions Regarding Minimum Duration of Breast-Feeding (in Months) for Boys and Girls

Table 5.3 shows that in Haryana with increasing female education and their exposure to mass media, children are getting more and more attention of their mothers. But the duration of breast-feeding in months for boys and girls as reported by respondents is decreasing. Nearly 70 per cent of women say that boys and girls should be fed for at least 12 months. However, only about 10 per cent women agreed on feeding boys and girls for 24 months. And the percentage of feeding beyond 24 months is very less.

**Table 5.3:** Haryana: Perceptions Regarding Duration of Breast-Feeding (in Months) for Boys and Girls

| *Duration of Breast-feeding* | *Percentage of Women* | |
|---|---|---|
| | *Boys* | *Girls* |
| 6 months | 12.3 | 18.5 |
| 12 months | 72.6 | 69.6 |
| 24 months | 11.4 | 10.5 |
| Above 24 months | 3.7 | 1.4 |

*Source*: Field Survey.

### 5.8 Exposure to Mass Media

In a country like India, where a large number of women are illiterate and have attained little or no formal school education, informal channels such as *mass media* plays an important role in bringing about modernization and thereby influencing and motivating women about their reproductive rights and choice.

As the level of education in Haryana is increasing both among male and female population, people are becoming aware of the importance of informal channels of education which play an important role in bringing modernization and influencing the day-to-day life and thinking about various rights and choices. Table 5.4 depicts that nearly 50 per cent of the population in all age-groups watches TV which has become a major source of information.

### 5.9 Perceptions on Family Size and Family Composition

The present study revealed that a large number of respondents (70.6 per cent) were of the opinion that women have a right to decide about the family size and only 25.1 per cent felt that it is not the women's right to decide family size and 4.3 per cent respondents said that they don't know whether women has right to decide family size or not (Table 5.5).

The perception of the majority of respondents (60.3 per cent) about ideal family size was two children followed by three children (21.5 per cent), one child (11.8 per cent), four children (6.1 per cent) and six children (0.3 per cent). Yadav and Badri (1997) found that most women considered three children as the ideal family size.

The ideal family composition as perceived by most of the respondents (58.7 per cent) included one boy and one girl. About 17.9 per cent of respondents considered two boys and one girl as the ideal family composition. 11.6 per cent respondents feel that there should be two boys in a family followed by 9.5 per cent as one boy being the ideal family size because it is too costly to brought-up a child and to give higher education and better living standard to him. The other responses included two girls and one boy (1.1 per cent). A negligible percentage (0.4 per cent) stated that they had no preference regarding the sex of the unborn baby.

**Table 5.4:** Haryana: Exposure of Respondents to Mass Media

| Age Group | Per cent of Respondents | | | | | | | |
|---|---|---|---|---|---|---|---|---|
| | *Only reads Newspaper* | *Only reads Magazine* | *Only watches TV* | *Read newspaper and magazine both* | *Read newspaper and watch TV* | *Read magazine and watch TV* | *Read newspaper and magazine and watch TV* | *Neither reads newspaper and magazine nor watches TV* |
| 15-19 | 4.3 | 2.6 | 46.1 | 5.7 | 21.2 | 12.6 | 6.7 | 0.8 |
| 20-24 | 5.5 | 3.4 | 50.4 | 5.8 | 17.0 | 14.1 | 3.6 | 0.2 |
| 25-29 | 3.4 | 2.9 | 61.3 | 1.3 | 11.5 | 12.9 | 5.1 | 1.6 |
| 30-34 | 2.3 | 3.6 | 47.8 | 2.9 | 15.3 | 11.7 | 15.7 | 0.7 |
| 35-39 | 6.4 | 2.4 | 42.0 | 2.3 | 16.8 | 9.4 | 20.4 | 0.3 |
| 40-44 | 7.2 | 1.6 | 51.5 | 1.9 | 18.3 | 7.9 | 11.2 | 0.4 |
| 45-49 | 7.9 | 1.2 | 58.7 | 1.1 | 20.2 | 3.1 | 6.7 | 1.1 |

*Source*: Field Survey

Table 5.5 also reveals, despite being educated, more than half i.e. 64.93 per cent of the respondents desired to have a son as their first born child, while 26.78 per cent respondents are of the opinion that it hardly matters whether first born child is son or daughter.

A trend to limit family size could be seen in respondents who were graduates and post-graduates, so that their children can enjoy higher standard of living by getting better educational facilities.

**Table 5.5:** Haryana: Respondents' Perception on Family Size and Composition

| *Perception on Family Size and Composition* | *Respondents (%)* |
|---|---|
| **Women's Right to Decide about Family Size** | |
| Have a right | 70.6 |
| No | 25.1 |
| Don't know | 4.3 |
| **Ideal Family Size** | |
| Two children | 60.3 |
| Three children | 21.5 |
| One child | 11.8 |
| Four | 6.1 |
| Six | 0.3 |
| **Ideal Family Composition** | |
| One boy and one girl | 58.7 |
| Two boys and one girl | 17.9 |
| Two boys | 11.6 |
| One boy | 9.5 |
| Two girls and one boy | 1.1 |
| Two girls | 0.8 |
| No preference for sex | 0.4 |
| **Preference for first born child** | |
| Son | 64.93 |
| Daughter | 8.29 |
| Son or Daughter, hardly matters | 26.78 |

*Source*: Field Survey.

The findings of the present study have also been substantiated by the studies made by Sangwan and Sangwan (2008), where 74.96 per cent of the respondents were desirous of having one son and one daughter as ideal family (Table 5.6); Anandalakshmy (1994) who found that more families have two sons (38.5 per cent) than two daughters (32 per cent); Srivastavā, Dasgupta and Rai, (2005) who found that about 5 per cent desired one child, the majority

(68.5 per cent) wanted two children, about 13.5 per cent desired three children and a negligible (3.5 per cent) were in favour of larger families; and NFHS-3, where seven out of 10 women and 8 out of 10 men consider the ideal family size to be two or fewer children. In Haryana, there is a strong preference for sons.

**Table 5.6:** Haryana: Composition of an Ideal Family

| *Response* | *No. of Respondents* | *Percentage* |
|---|---|---|
| **What is ideal family?** | | |
| Two Sons and Two Daughters | 82 | 6.11 |
| Two Sons and One Daughter | 188 | 14.01 |
| One Son and One Daughter | 1006 | 74.96 |
| One Son and Two Daughters | 66 | 4.92 |
| **Total** | **1342** | **100.00** |

*Source:* Sangwan and Sangwan (2008).

Twenty-two per cent of women and 18 per cent of men want more sons than daughters, but only 1-2 per cent of women and men want more daughters than sons. However, most men and women would like to have at least one son and at least one daughter. In Haryana, unplanned pregnancies are relatively common. If all women were to have only the number of children they wanted, the total fertility rate would have already reached the replacement level of 2.1 children per woman instead of the current level of 2.7 children per woman.

## 5.10 Perceptions of the Respondents about Dowry

The perception of respondents was noticed about dowry in the villages surveyed. It was found that 23.8 per cent respondents feel that dowry is essential for girl to start a family without any kind of difficulty. They feel that when we are giving comforts to girl at our home, all those things should be available to her in '*Sasural*' also. Middle class people whose economic condition is not very good think that dowry is a major problem, this type of respondents were 60.5 per cent in present study. Only 15.7 per cent respondents were of the view that it is a right to men to demand and accept dowry (Table 5.7).

**Table 5.7:** Haryana: Perceptions of Respondents about Dowry

| *Perceptions of Respondents about Dowry* | *Respondents (Percentage)* |
|---|---|
| A major problem | 60.5 |
| Essential to start a family | 23.8 |
| Right of a man | 15.7 |

*Source:* Field Survey.

## 5.11 Perception about Minimum Money to be Spent on the Marriage of a Daughter

It is general perception that the marriage of a daughter is a costlier affair which is revealed in this field survey. A total of 93.7 per cent of the respondents said that there is existence of dowry system.

Table 5.8 gives the minimum amount of money to be spent on the marriage of a daughter. A total of 78.2 per cent respondents answered this question that each and every household item is becoming too costly that simple marriage is not possible without a minimum amount of Rs. 5 lakhs. About one-sixth of respondents (17.7 per cent) said that the minimum amount to be spent on marriage of a daughter is Rs. 3 to 5 lakh followed by 3.2 per cent respondents who spent Rs. 1 to 3 lakh, and only 0.9 per cent spent up to Rs. 1 lakh on the marriage of daughter.

**Table 5.8:** Haryana: Perception of Respondents about Minimum Money to be Spent on the Marriage of a Daughter

| *Perceptions about Dowry* | *Respondents (Percentage)* |
|---|---|
| **Existence of Dowry** | |
| Yes | 97.3 |
| No | 2.7 |
| **Amount of Money Spent on the Marriage of a Daughter** | |
| Up to Rs. 1,00,000 | 0.9 |
| Rs. 1,00,000 to Rs. 3,00,000 | 3.2 |
| Rs. 3,00,000 to Rs. 5,00,000 | 17.7 |
| More than Rs. 5,00,000 | 78.2 |
| **Source of Arranging Money for Marriage** | |
| Savings | 63.6 |
| Loan | 25.9 |
| Selling of property | 10.5 |

*Source:* Field Survey.

Most of the respondents (63.6 per cent) arranged the money for marriage of their daughter from their savings. They said when a daughter's birth takes place in the family she become a liability for them and they know her marriage will bring a lot of financial burden on them so they start saving some money for her marriage. On the other hand, 25.9 per cent respondents arranged the money by taking loan from banks, from *sahukars,* etc. and only 10.5 per cent respondents sell their property for a respectable marriage of their daughter. Moreover, some of them feel that it is a right of daughter to share the property of parents.

## 5.12 Family Planning

### *5.12.1 Knowledge of Family Planning Methods*

During the field survey it is revealed that most of the respondents were aware of the family planning methods, these facilities are made available to them by *anganwadi* workers, ANMs, in primary health centres, etc. Knowledge of contraception is almost universal in Haryana. Female sterilization is the most widely known method. Adults are less likely to know about temporary contraceptive methods. The government family planning programme promotes three temporary methods: the pill, the IUD, and condoms. Of these three methods, currently married women are most likely to know about the pill (90 per cent) and currently married men are most likely to know about condoms (95 per cent). Knowledge of female sterilization has been high since NFHS-1, but knowledge of male sterilization has decreased since NFHS-1. Knowledge of temporary contraceptive methods has also decreased in the last seven years.

Knowledge of pills, IUDs, and condoms among currently married women decreased by 4-7 percentage points between NFHS-2 and NFHS-3, after increasing between NFHS-1 and NFHS-2. Almost two-thirds of currently married women in Haryana are using contraception, mainly female sterilization. Only 43 per cent of users of modern contraceptive methods were told by a health or family planning worker about other methods they could use. (NFHS-3, Haryana State Report, 2008)

### 5.12.2 Delivery Care

Nearly two-thirds of births (64 per cent) take place at home and 36 per cent take place in a health facility. However, the percentage of births in a health facility has increased substantially over time, from 18 per cent in NFHS-1 and 22 per cent in NFHS-2 to 39 per cent in NFHS-3. Institutional births are more common among women who have received antenatal check-ups, women with 10 or more years of education, women who are having their first birth, women in the highest wealth quintile, Sikh women, and women who do not belong to Scheduled Castes, Scheduled Tribes, or Other Backward Classes. For 82 per cent of home births, a clean blade was used to cut the cord, as is recommended. A disposable delivery kit was used for 72 per cent of deliveries. Eighty-five per cent of home births followed the recommendation that the baby be immediately wiped dry and then wrapped without being bathed first. Half of births (49 per cent) during the past five years took place with assistance from a health professional, and another half of births were delivered by a traditional birth attendant.

Fifteen per cent of children had health check-ups at an *anganwadi* centre and 9 per cent of children received growth monitoring services. However, mothers in Haryana breast-feed for an average of 26 months, which is slightly longer than the minimum of 24 months recommended by WHO for most children.

## 5.13 Awareness of Respondents about the MTP Act, PNDT Act, Declining Sex Ratio and Place of Sex Determination Tests

Table 5.9 gives us information about the respondent's knowledge about MTP Act, PNDT Act and declining sex ratio in Haryana. About 95 per cent respondents were not aware about the existence of these Acts. However, 92.1 per cent respondents were aware about the fact that there is a shortage of girls in Haryana. Though, the respondents don't know about the MTP and PNDT Acts, but they were well equipped with the information about the availability of places for sex determination tests and clinics for termination of pregnancy if the sex is determined as girl. 87.4 per cent respondents were found aware of this type of facility located in urban areas. But they were hesitant enough to the locations of such clinics as it is illegal and for such a crime there is punishment also. No one among the respondents accepted that they themselves have undergone any such tests.

**Table 5.9:** Haryana: Awareness of Respondents about the MTP Act, PNDT Act, Declining Sex Ratio and Place of Sex Determination Tests

| *Awareness of Respondents about the MTP Act, PNDT Act, Declining Sex Ratio and Place of Sex Determination Tests* | *Respondents (%)* |
|---|---|
| **Awareness about the MTP Act** | |
| Aware | 3.7 |
| Not aware | 96.3 |
| **Awareness about PNDT Act** | |
| Aware | 5.2 |
| Not Aware | 94.8 |
| **Awareness about Declining Sex Ratio** | |
| Aware | 92.1 |
| Not Aware | 7.9 |
| **Awareness about Place of Sex Determination Tests** | |
| Aware | 87.4 |
| Not Aware | 12.6 |

*Source:* Field Survey.

## 5.14 Awareness and Perception of Women about Abortion and Abortion Related Issues

In a study conducted by Nayar (1995), all the respondents in both Punjab and Haryana were aware of sonography as a method of sex determination.

None of them were aware of other methods. The majority were not in favour of getting sex determination tests (Srivastava, Dasgupta and Rai, 2005). Prasad (2001) found that it was the family's decision to undergo the sex determination test while the mothers stated that it was not a forced decision, as they wanted to give birth to a male child. Most of the respondents (83.5 per cent) felt that the decision to undergo an abortion should rest with the prospective parents; some felt that the prospective mother should take it and only a negligible percentage (5 per cent) felt that other members of the family should take the decision.

# 6 Declining Juvenile Sex-Ratio

## Issues and Concerns

Census 2001 figures showed that the child sex ratio in India, which had become a concern in the 1991 census, has gone down even further—from 945 in 1991 to 927 in 2001. States such as Punjab, Haryana, Himachal Pradesh, Chandigarh and Delhi now have fewer than 900 girls per 1,000 boys.

Out of the total population (2,11,44,564) of Haryana, the population in 0-6 years age-group is 33,35,537 and the sex ratio of this age-group is 820 female children per 1000 male children, which is not a good sign for the future. While in 1991, not a single district of Haryana recorded sex ratio of less than 800, in 2001, Kurukshetra, Ambala, Sonipat, Kaithal, and Rohtak districts recorded figures less than 800 (Table 6.1 and Fig. 6.1).

Viewed in its regional perspective, the child sex ratio in Haryana varies greatly from one part of the state to another. Out of the total of 19 districts, 8 districts display sex ratio more than the state average of 819 females per 1000 males. In other words, about half of the total districts recorded sex ratio above the state's average, but all the districts are having sex ratio below the national average of 927 females per 1000 males. It means the whole of Haryana is characterized with excessive deficiency of females.

Gurgaon district of southern Haryana has the highest sex ratio of 858 females per 1000 males. It is followed by Faridabad district (850). Both the districts are coming up fast as potential industrial areas and have made their place on the industrial map of Haryana.

The other districts, which are having child sex ratio above the state's average (819 females per 1000 males), are Bhiwani (841),

Hisar (832), Panchkula (829), Fatehabad (828), Jind (818) and Mahendragarh (818).

**Table 6.1:** Haryana: Child Sex Ratio by Descending Order of Districts, 2001

| *State/District* | *Females Per 1000 Males* |
|---|---|
| **Haryana** | **819** |
| Gurgaon | 858 |
| Faridabad | 850 |
| Bhiwani | 841 |
| Hisar | 832 |
| Panchkula | 829 |
| Fatehabad | 828 |
| Jind | 818 |
| Mahendragarh | 818 |
| Sirsa | 817 |
| Rewari | 811 |
| Karnal | 809 |
| Panipat | 809 |
| Yamunanagar | 806 |
| Jhajjar | 801 |
| Rohtak | 799 |
| Kaithal | 791 |
| Sonipat | 788 |
| Ambala | 782 |
| Kurukshetra | 771 |

*Source:* Census of India (2001), *Haryana, Population Data Sheet-District-wise*, Directorate of Census Operations, Haryana, Chandigarh, p. 4.

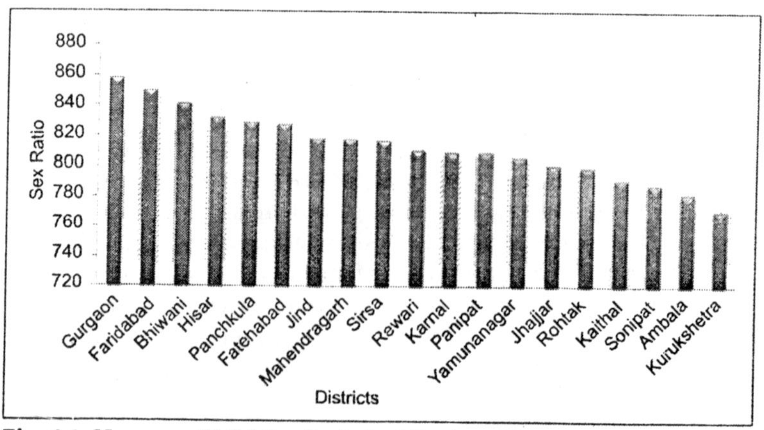


**Fig. 6.1:** Haryana: Child Sex Ratio by Districts, 2001.

At the other end of the scale, Kurukshetra district, the pious land of Mahabharata, has the lowest sex ratio of 771 females per 1000 males. Kurukshetra district is followed by the districts of Ambala (782), Sonipat (788), Kaithal (791), and Rohtak (799).

## 6.1 Rural-Urban Differentials in Child Sex Ratio

*Rural-urban break up* of child sex ratio indicates that out of the total of 19 districts in Haryana, 16 districts have rural sex ratio higher than the urban (Table 6.2).

Gurgaon district has the highest rural child sex ratio of 866 females per 1000 males and is followed by the adjoining district of Faridabad with 851 females per 1000 males.

The other districts which have rural child sex ratio higher than the urban are characterised with relatively low rural child sex ratio of less than 850 females per 1000 males. But extremely low rural child sex ratio of less than 800 females per 1000 males is experienced by only three districts. Ambala district with 770 females per 1000 males stands at the lowest and is followed by the districts of Kurukshetra (773) and Sonipat (792).

The striking deficiency of females in these districts has been explained by: (i) availability of better educational facilities, and (ii) increasing trend of female foeticide due to easy access to sex-selective technology.

By comparison, out of the total of 19 districts in Haryana, only 3 districts of Rewari (816), Ambala (808), and Jhajjar (804) have experienced urban child sex ratio higher than their rural counterpart.

The higher urban child sex ratio is mainly due to the family migration to urban areas either on getting job or for the attainment of education for their children, greater survival rate of both males and females because of the availability of better medical facilities. Moreover, attitudinal change in urban society leading to somewhat greater attention towards girl child in recent years also increased urban child sex ratio to some extent.

The rural-urban differentials in child sex ratio in India were the result of sex-selectivity among the rural-urban migrants in the past. More males than females moved from rural to urban areas. Such a rural-urban migration takes place due to push and pull forces operating in the two areas. However, the male-selective influx into urban areas is the result of—(i) prejudice against female employment and mobility, (ii) scarcity of jobs suitable for females, and (iii) high cost of living and problem of housing in urban centres which discourage and compel many male migrants to leave their families behind. Moreover, the joint family system prevailing in rural areas facilitates male-selective migration as the male migrant is assured of the safety and security of his family left behind (Krishan and Chandna, 1973). Thus, the rural-urban differential in sex ratio was largely the product of male-selectivity in rural-urban migration. This explanation is also relevant in the case of Haryana.

Jind district has the highest rural-urban differential (+53) in the child sex ratio and is followed by the districts of Gurgaon (+50),

**Table 6.2:** Haryana: Child Sex Ratio by Rural-Urban Residence, 2001

| *State/District* | *Females Per 1000 Males* | | *Rural-Urban Differential* |
|---|---|---|---|
| | *Rural* | *Urban* | |
| **Haryana** | **823** | **808** | **+15** |
| Jind | 828 | 775 | +53 |
| Gurgaon | 866 | 816 | +50 |
| Fatehabad | 834 | 798 | +36 |
| Hisar | 839 | 806 | +33 |
| Kaithal | 796 | 769 | +27 |
| Panchkula | 839 | 813 | +26 |
| Rohtak | 807 | 781 | +26 |
| Mahendragarh | 821 | 795 | +26 |
| Yamunanagar | 814 | 789 | +25 |
| Sirsa | 823 | 801 | +22 |
| Karnal | 813 | 792 | +21 |
| Sonipat | 792 | 775 | +17 |
| Bhiwani | 844 | 827 | +17 |
| Kurukshetra | 773 | 766 | +6 |
| Panipat | 810 | 807 | +3 |
| Faridabad | 851 | 848 | +3 |
| Jhajjar * | 800 | 804 | -4 |
| Rewari* | 810 | 816 | -6 |
| Ambala* | 770 | 808 | -38 |

*Source:* Census of India (2001), *Haryana, Population Data Sheet-District Wise*, Directorate of Census Operations, Haryana, Chandigarh, pp. 10-46.

* The districts with higher urban sex ratio than rural.

*Note:* The districts have been arranged in descending order of rural-urban differential.

Fatehabad (+36), Hisar (+33), Kaithal (+27), Panchkula (+26), Rohtak (+26), and Mahendragarh (+26).

On the other hand, Faridabad district has the lowest rural-urban differential (+3) in the child sex ratio and is followed by the districts of Panipat (+3) and Kurukshetra (+6). The narrowing down of rural-urban differential signifies the increasing trend toward family type rural-urban migration which in turn stems from: (i) increased social approval of out-of-home female mobility, (ii) large number of avenues for female employment in urban areas, and (iii) the recently increased trend towards nuclear families.

Negative rural-urban differential in child sex ratio is found only in three districts of Ambala (-38), Rewari (-6), and Jhajjar (-4) and is mainly due to attitudinal change in urban society leading to somewhat greater attention towards girl child and greater survival rate of both males and females because of the availability of better medical facilities.

According to SRS Bulletin 2005, the total crude death rate in India is 8.0 but female crude death rate is 7.5 which is lower than the male crude death rate (8.4). Again, this crude death rate is much lower in urban (6.0) than rural (8.7) areas. Even in the urban areas female crude death rate (5.4) is further lower than male crude death rate (6.4).

These trends of death rate by sex and residence are similar and even lower in economically better performing state of Haryana.

The female crude death rate in Haryana is 6.0 which is lower than male crude death rate (8.0). But it is much lower in urban population (5.5) than in rural folk (6.1).

If this is so then why is sex ratio declining? The answer is simple that either the girls are not allowed to be born or female foeticide is rampant in urban areas. As a result, sex ratio is declining more in urban population than in rural areas.

Statistical figures of infant mortality rate (IMR) by sex and residence provided by SRS 2005 are very much crucial to understand the process and dynamics of sex ratio declining in the state of Haryana.

At this point of time, national IMR is 60. In case of males, it is 57 and for females it is 64. In rural areas, female IMR (69) is more than the male IMR (63). Even in the urban areas, female IMR (44) is more than the male IMR (33).

These patterns of urban female IMR figures are indicative of dangerous implications in the so-called economically better performing states like Haryana. The total IMR in the state of Haryana is 59, while it is 61 in rural and 49 in urban areas. But there is a huge difference of IMR between males (54) and females (65). Even in rural areas, the difference between both the IMRs for males (56) and females (67) is large. The same is also true in case of urban areas. The IMR is 43 for males and 56 for females. However, infant mortality rate by sex clearly indicates the trend of why sex ratio is getting imbalanced in the economically progressive states like Haryana.

In Haryana, the total IMR is 11 points more in females than in males, which is almost same in both rural (11 points) and urban (13 points) areas, while it is only 7 points at the national level.

From these figures it can be stated that female foeticide is more in urban areas, which creates vulnerable conditions for urban sex ratio.

## 6.2 Causes of Declining Juvenile Sex Ratio

The causes responsible for the declining juvenile sex ratio as perceived by the respondents of the study are presented in Table 6.3 and Fig. 6.2. The dominating causes responsible were son preference and dowry. As 46.3 per cent respondents said that son preference is main cause and the other 21.6 per cent said that dowry is the main reason for not giving birth to a girl child. The interesting finding is that the mushrooming of private nursing homes/clinics with ultrasound facilities and the ability to pay for abortions were also articulated by a large number of respondents as important contributing causes. Poor implementation of the various Acts and laws was also mentioned as one of the causes. However, it was not viewed as a major contributing factor for declining juvenile sex ratio.

### *6.2.1 Son Preference*

The son preference is considered as the leading cause of declining juvenile sex ratio, because couples desire to have a male child for the continuation of their family tree, to support them in their old age and to perform last rituals.

**Table 6.3:** Haryana: Causes Responsible for the Declining Juvenile Sex Ratio as Perceived by the Respondents

| *Causes* | *Respondents* | *Percentage* |
|---|---|---|
| Son Preference | 5,258 | 46.3 |
| Dowry | 2,453 | 21.6 |
| Poor implementation of MTP, dowry law, etc. | 239 | 2.1 |
| Mushrooming of ultrasound clinics | 613 | 5.4 |
| Easy accessibility of Technology for Sex selection | 704 | 6.2 |
| Ability to pay for abortion | 352 | 3.1 |
| Feeling of Insecurity of a Girl Child | 886 | 7.8 |
| Female Foeticide/Sex selective Abortions | 727 | 6.4 |
| Crime against Women | 363 | 3.2 |
| Negligence among Women about their Health | 125 | 1.1 |
| **Total** | **11,357** | **100.00** |

*Source*: Field Survey.

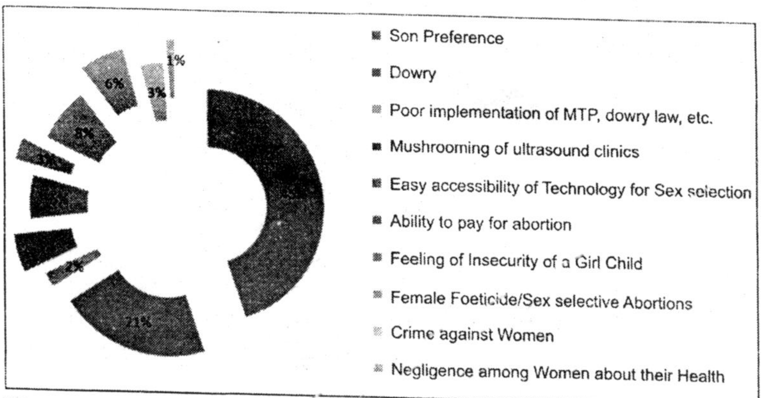


**Fig. 6.2:** Haryana: Causes Responsible for the Declining Juvenile Sex Ratio as Perceived by the Respondents

It has been corroborated by the studies made by Sangwan and Sangwan (2008) where 53.05 per cent of respondents considered son preference as the dominating cause of declining juvenile sex ratio. Reasons for son preference were that they carry on the family name and inherit property; they are support providers in old age and perform the last rites (MOHFW and TINNARI, 2002). The reason for wanting a son is to attain *moksha* (Prasad, 2001; and Nayar, 1995); power, prestige, to perform the last rites and continuing the family lineage (Yadav and Badri, 1997).

**Table 6.4:** Haryana: Reasons for Son Preference

| Sr. No. | Reasons for Son Preference | Respondents (Per cent) |
|---|---|---|
| 1. | Carries on the family name | 56.3 |
| 2. | He is a support provider in old age | 18.9 |
| 3. | For performing the last rites | 13.2 |
| 4. | Brings in dowry instead of draining family resources | 7.1 |
| 5. | Wealth remains in the family | 4.5 |

*Source:* Field Survey.

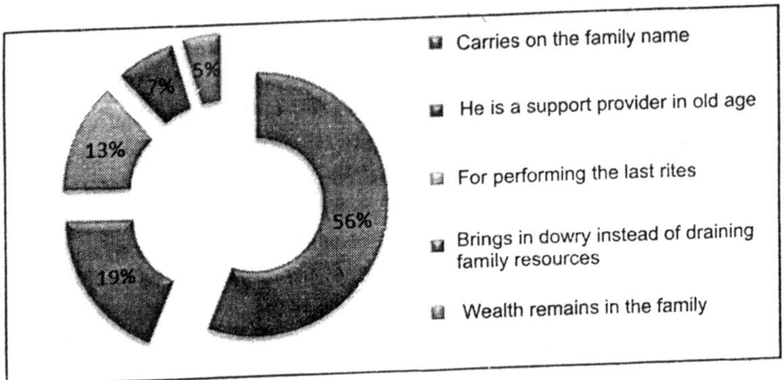


**Fig. 6.3:** Haryana: Reasons for Son Preference.

It is very much clear from Table 6.4 and Fig 6.3 that more than 50 per cent of the total respondents are of the view that son carries the family name. Among 18.9 per cent respondents' son preference is for getting support in old age followed by 13.2 per cent with a feeling that the last rituals can only be performed by the boy to get *Moksha.* A total of 7.1 per cent respondents think in economic terms and said that a boy brings in dowry instead of draining the family resources and only 4.5 per cent respondents said that with investments on sons, say on education or business, the wealth remains in the family. Thus, the findings reveal that among the society, a deep-seated mindset of son preference still exists for perpetuating the family name and performing the last rites and rituals.

### 6.2.2 Son Preference and Abortion

Abortion can be linked to son preference in two ways. First, the prevalence of abortions may differ according to the sex of the living children in the family, even if the sex of the foetus is not known. Secondly, sex selective abortions may be used to avoid birth of child of an undesired sex after the sex of the foetus has been determined. The following analysis shows whether abortion in Haryana is related to son preference or not.

During data collection, it was observed that there is a clandestine practice of aborting female foetus in Haryana through the use of ultrasound technique in private clinics. Female foetus is aborted after three and half months when the sex of the foetus becomes recognizable as reported by doctors. During the last few years, cases of abortion have increased significantly and people of rural areas are flocking in large numbers for induced abortions. The cost of abortion ranges from Rs. 2000 to Rs. 5000 depending upon the client's status as well as the status of the clinic. It has been reported by the doctors that a couple with one or two daughters mostly go for abortions, as they don't want additional daughters. However, abortion is rarely resorted to in respect with the first child and even the birth of first daughter is tolerated.

Some of the villagers openly admitted that they are aborting female foetus, because it is very difficult to get their daughter married to a suitable boy. They consider them a liability. Some villagers who were desirous of male child are also duped by few footloose doctors by giving some tablets or injections to the women on the pretext that a male child will be born to them.

The Pre-Natal Diagnostic Technique (PNDT) Act, 1994, is mostly flouted. This has accentuated recently because of the factors, such as, proximity of towns to villages in the wake of increasing accessibility by roads.

### *6.2.3 Social Evil of Dowry Associated with the Marriage of the Girls*

Dowry normally means gifts given during the marriage to the son–in–law or his parents either in cash or kind. From the point of view of women's status, however, dowry has to be looked at as constituting what is given to the bride, and is often settled before hand. The gifts, though given to the bride, may not be regarded as exclusively her property, but includes what is given to the bridegroom before and after marriage; and what is presented to the in-laws of the girl. The practice of giving dowry is meant to assist a newly-wed couple to start their life together with ease. However, now it has degenerated into a sordid commercial transaction in which monetary considerations receive priority over the personal merits of the bride.

It is a deep-rooted instinct of the culture of Haryana that girl is always considered as a *Paraya Dhan*. Moreover, there is thinking among the respondents that a large amount is required for her marriage. Whether, she is educated or not, to get a good bridegroom it requires a lot of money in the form of dowry. If girl is educated, the problem becomes even worse, because *'higher the education, higher the expenditure on marriage to maintain the status'*. Even after marriage, girls in Haryana remain liability towards parents and brothers in the form of gifts (*Siddha* and *Kothli*) on various festivals every year and in the form of *Sindhara* (on the occasion of 1st *Teej* festival after marriage), *Pillia* (on the birth of a baby), *Chhucchhak* (when after delivery she visits her *Mayka*), *Bhaat* (at the time of her children's marriage). She remains burden on parental family till the end of her life.

Thus, it is a universal truth that 'dowry' is essential during marriage of a girl whether it has taken on a negative connotation or a corrupt form of social custom related to the marriage. Therefore, marriages continue to take place and dowry, whether demanded or given willingly, continues to accompany the newly-wed bride to her in-laws home. It is unthinkable that a bride can go to her husband's home, without taking anything in the form of dowry. Hence, dowry continues to be an integral part of the society. That is why, people prefer to give birth to a boy instead of a girl because girls take dowry while sons bring in a substantial amount of dowry. More investment on girls in the form of their education is thought to be unnecessary, because even if they earn, parents in Haryana are not willing to expend that money on them. They think that the *'use of earnings of a girl is a sinful act'* on the part of parents. It can be used by in-laws only. Thus, rising demand for dowry makes daughters financial burdens.

Data presented in Table 6.5 and Fig. 6.4 provides an understanding of the views of respondents regarding the prevalence and magnitude of dowry in the state. Whether it is northern or southern region; eastern or western region, it was found that dowry is being practiced widely throughout the state irrespective of economic status, religion or caste. In Haryana, only 15.1 per cent people agreed that the dowry is declining in the state. 2.5 per cent preferred not responding either way. A large number of respondents (82.4 per cent) disagreed with this and said the trend of dowry has not decreased so far, but has, in fact, increased over the years correlated it with wealth of people.

**Table 6.5:** Haryana: Respondents' views on Prevalence of Dowry in the State

| *Responses* | *Respondents* | *Percentage* |
|---|---|---|
| Increase in Dowry | 9,358 | 82.4 |
| Decrease in Dowry | 1,715 | 15.1 |
| Don't know | 284 | 2.5 |
| **Total** | **11,357** | **100.00** |

*Source:* Field Survey.

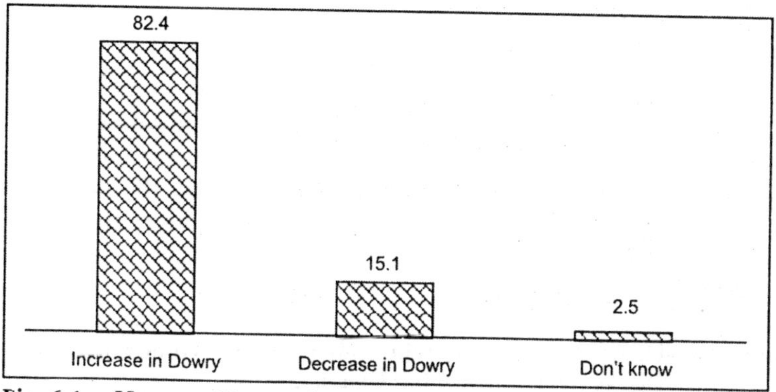


**Fig. 6.4:** Haryana: Respondents' Views on Prevalence of Dowry in the State.

### 6.2.4 *Dowry and Female Foeticide*

The dowry system has always given rise to innumerable socio-economic problems of far-reaching consequences and wide-ranging ramification. It is said that in India, on an average, five women a day are burnt in dowry-related disputes and many cases are never reported. It is well-known that legislation by itself cannot normally solve deep-rooted social problems. Nonetheless, legislation is necessary to exercise educative impact besides providing legal sanctions against this social evil of devastating consequences. Therefore, female foeticide is intrinsically linked to the dowry system. To eliminate female foeticide, it is essential to end the ritual of dowry.

### 6.2.5 *Easy Accessibility of Technology for Sex Selection*

*Sonography*

In the present study, there were 15,345 currently-married women. They had children but none of them directly revealed that they had ever gone for sonography, although the figures shown by *The Tribune*, New Delhi, Tuesday, January 24, 2012, shows that the PNDT Act, is being violated and the Board of Governors of Medical Council of India is directed to cancel licenses of all 93 doctors convicted for sex determination of foetuses under the Pre-Conception and Pre-Natal Diagnostic Techniques, 1966.

*Decision-Making for Sonography*

Table 6.6 and Fig. 6.5 shows that decision to undergo sonography in the state of Haryana by 74.3 per cent respondents was taken by husband and in-laws followed by 12.7 per cent by the woman herself. Another 7.1 per cent had not mentioned the decision at all. Women mostly had undergone this test around 12 to 15 weeks of gestation of pregnancy.

**Table 6.6:** Haryana: Person(s) who Motivated the Women to Take Decision for Undergoing Ultrasound Test

| *Person(s) who motivated the women for Ultrasound Test* | *Respondents* | *Percentage* |
|---|---|---|
| Self | 1,949 | 12.7 |
| Husband/In Laws | 11,401 | 74.3 |
| Doctor/ANMs/Nurses | 905 | 5.9 |
| Not Stated | 1,090 | 7.1 |
| **Total** | **15,345** | **100.00** |

*Source*: Field Survey.

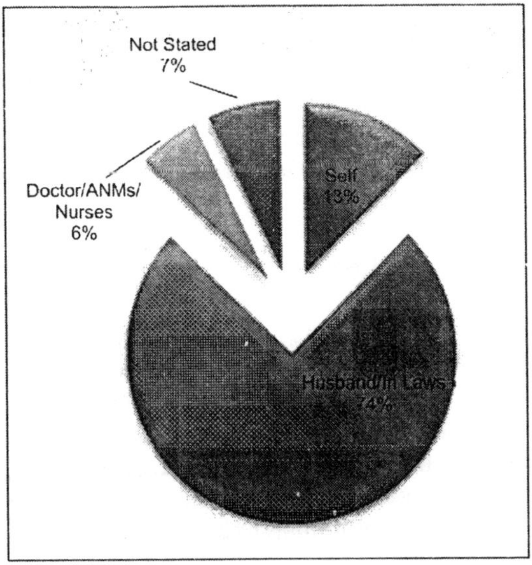


**Fig. 6.5:** Haryana: Persons who Motivated the Women to take Decision for undergoing Ultrasound Test.

According to NFHS-3, the use of ultrasound is much more common in Haryana than in India as a whole (24 per cent). Women with at least 10 years of education were more than four times as likely to have an ultrasound test as women with no education. Only 6 per cent of births among women in the lowest wealth quintile had an ultrasound test, compared with 66 per cent of births among women in the highest wealth quintile. Pregnant women with no living son are much more likely to have an ultrasound test than those with at least one son.

### 6.3 Status of the Girl Child and Women's Empowerment

Women's autonomy is likely to have a significant impact on the demographic and health-seeking behaviour of couples, by altering their relative control over fertility and contraceptive use, and by influencing their attitudes and abilities. The NFHS-3 (2005-06) revealed that about 41 per cent of women report that they make their own decision on how they use the money they earn. About 30 per cent of women reported that their husbands or other members of the family, along with their husbands, took the decisions.

Freedom of movement outside the home is an important aspect of women's autonomy and empowerment. NFHS-3 (2005-06) found that only 33 per cent of women were allowed to go alone to the market, a health facility or places outside the village and about 4 per cent were not allowed to go out at all to any of these places (IIPS, 2007).

### *6.3.1 Decision-Making Abilities of Women in Family*

The power of decision-making among the families of Haryana normally lies in the hands of the head of the household. Majority of the head of the households are male folks. Moreover, after them, the decisions about wife and children are used to be taken by husbands. Even if, the education level of female in Haryana is increasing, they are going outside home for jobs to earn money, yet only a small fraction of women indulge in the family decisions such as:

- Education of the Children;
- Taking the Child to Health Facilities when he/she is suffering from illness;
- Seeking Health Care for Self;
- Buying Clothes or Jewellery for Self;
- Decision to Go and Stay with Parents or Siblings;
- Decision on How to Spend the Money Earned by the Women;
- Decision of where the brother-in-law or sister-in-law will be married and to whom; and
- Decision for selling and buying of Property.

## 6.4 Reasons for Undergoing Ultrasound

All those women who had undergone ultrasound, some questions were asked to know why they had undergone ultrasound. Table 6.7 and Fig. 6.6 shows that in case of Haryana, 34 per cent respondents have said that they wanted to know the sex of the child. Majority of the respondents reported that they wanted to know the baby's health, which looks dubious. Except abnormalities and position of baby (to know the position of baby, test is conducted after 7 months of gestation), all other reasons look defensive.

**Table 6.7:** Haryana: Reasons for Ultrasound

| *Reasons* | *Respondents* | *Percentage* |
|---|---|---|
| Sex of Child | 3,918 | 34.5 |
| Position of Baby | 591 | 5.2 |
| Child's Health | 3,714 | 32.7 |
| Abnormality | 556 | 4.9 |
| Mother's Health | 1,772 | 15.6 |
| Not Stated | 806 | 7.1 |
| **Total** | **11,357** | **100.00** |

*Source*: Field Survey.

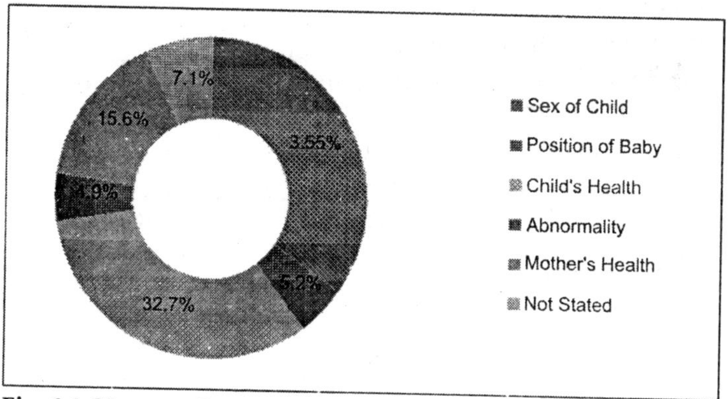


**Fig. 6.6:** Haryana: Reasons for Ultrasound.

## 6.5 Female Foeticide/Sex Selective Abortions and Related Issues

The three major reasons for terminating pregnancy found in almost all studies are to avoid an additional birth after the desired family size had been achieved; to ensure a reasonable birth interval after the previous birth; and to prevent the birth of a female child. A majority of the women respondents (62 per cent) had undergone induced abortion because they did not want another child. The majority were in the higher income group. One-fourth reported that they only wanted a son. Most of the respondents were reluctant to disclose the place of abortion. Of these, more than half admitted using a private clinic for the purpose and less than 40 per cent had used government facilities. In Haryana, *dais* also conducted abortions on a small scale. Moreover, advertisements through mass media are also one of the factors for playing an important role in terminating the pregnancy within specified period of conception. Many types of pills are also suggested through these advertisements to stop the birth of unwanted sex.

### *6.5.1 Places of Induced Abortion*

Table 6.8 and Fig. 6.7 provide information about the places where induced abortion took place among the ever–married and currently married women of Haryana according to the order of pregnancy.

**Table 6.8:** Haryana: Health Facilities where Induced Abortions Took Place among Women

| *Health Facility* | *Respondents* | *Percentage* |
|---|---|---|
| Private Clinic | 7,768 | 68.4 |
| Government Hospitals | 2,783 | 24.5 |
| Others | 806 | 7.1 |
| **Total** | **11,357** | **100.00** |

*Source*: Field Survey.

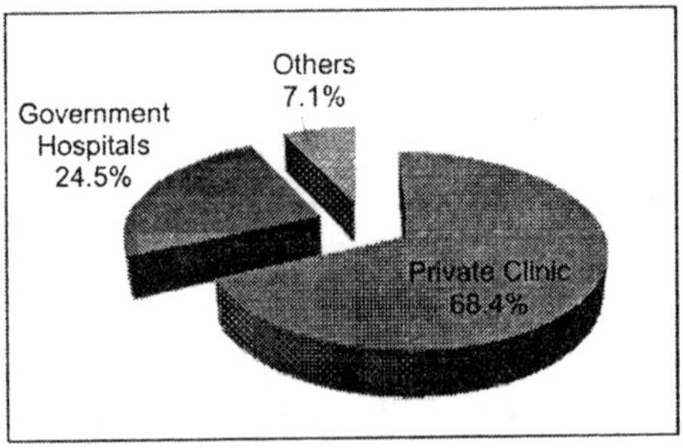


**Fig. 6.7:** Haryana: Health Facilities where Induced Abortions Took Place among Women.

Table 6.8 shows that 68.4 per cent respondents were of the opinion that the maximum number of induced abortions in Haryana has taken place in private clinics. However, according to 24.5 per cent respondents induced abortions took place in government hospitals in the form of MTP because if continuing:

- the pregnancy poses a risk to the pregnant women;
- there is a danger of the baby being handicapped;

- there is a risk of a baby born with mental abnormalities;
- the pregnancy resulted from rape; and
- the pregnancy has occurred as a result of the failure of family planning methods.

Only 7.1 per cent respondents were of the view that such acts are being done by other channels, i.e. ANM, non-trained *dais*, trained *dais*, pharmacist, etc.

However, women are taking a great risk by getting abortions done through *dais* at home, exposing themselves to greater risks of infection and death. Probably, it is the desire for a son that forces women to adopt such a risky step. In nutshell, private clinics seem to be more preferred places for terminating pregnancy than the government hospitals in the study area.

### *6.5.2 Causes for Terminating Pregnancy*

The various causes for terminating pregnancy include: limiting family size; birth spacing; the foetus was not developing well; and heavy bleeding, so to avoid any further complication (Table 6.9 and Fig. 6.8).

**Table 6.9:** Haryana: Causes for Terminating Pregnancy

| *Reasons for Terminating Pregnancy* | *Respondents* | *Percentage* |
|---|---|---|
| Limiting family size | 6,121 | 53.9 |
| Do not want girl child | 2,068 | 18.2 |
| Birth Spacing | 1,749 | 15.4 |
| Foetus was not developing well | 920 | 8.1 |
| Heavy bleeding | 363 | 3.2 |
| Early conception | 136 | 1.2 |
| **Total** | **11,357** | **100.00** |

*Source:* Field Survey.

Majority of the respondents (53.9 per cent) said that the main cause for terminating pregnancy is for achieving the limited family size followed by 18.2 per cent with the reason that they do not want a girl child and 15.4 per cent respondents were of the view that birth spacing is one of the causes for abortion (Table 6.9 and Fig. 6.8).

While explaining reasons for increasing trend of female foeticide among married female teachers of reproductive age randomly selected from various schools, colleges and universities of Haryana, Sangwan and Sangwan (2008) gave the following order of preference as per responses of the respondents which are mentioned in Table 6.10.

**Table 6.10:** Main Reasons (in Preferential Order) for Increasing Trend of Female Foeticide in Haryana

| *Responses* | *Respondents* | *Percentage* |
|---|---|---|
| The desire of couples to have a male child for the continuation of their family tree and to support them in their old age. | 712 | 53.05 |
| Sex-Selective Abortions (SSAs) because of availability of technology for sex detection of the unborn child in abundance. | 276 | 20.57 |
| Money-power of people to pay for the sex-selective technology and easy access to the clinics available in abundance because of improved infrastructure | 135 | 10.06 |
| The rising demand for dowry that makes daughters financial burden on parents | 93 | 6.93 |
| The girl is considered as *Praya Dhan*, because she grows and settles in her husband's household after marriage. | 79 | 5.89 |
| The feeling of insecurity of a girl child | 47 | 3.50 |
| **Total** | **1,342** | **100.00** |

*Source*: Sangwan and Sangwan (2008).

Table 6.10 reveals that more than half of the total respondents consider that the most important reason for increasing trend of female foeticide in Haryana is the desire of couples to have a male child for the continuation of their family tree and to support them in their old age. It is followed by Sex-Selective Abortions (SSAs) because of availability of technology for sex detection of the unborn child in abundance

Moreover, people have money-power to pay for the technology and of course, as infrastructure improved, people could access the clinics easily. In addition to this, the rising demand for dowry, consideration of girls as *Praya Dhan* and the feeling of insecurity of a girl child have made foeticide rampant in Haryana.

According to various observations during field survey, respondents explained about some more causes for not wanting a girl child. These are:

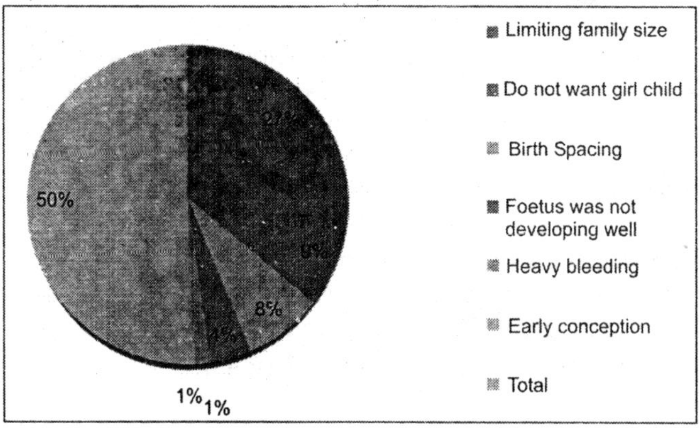


**Fig. 6.8:** Haryana: Causes for Terminating Pregnancy

### *6.5.3 Feeling of Insecurity of a Girl Child*

One of the basic reasons rooted in the thoughts of society for not wanting a girl child is insecurity which is spreading in the form of a nuisance in the society. Initially it was thought that a girl is secure when she is married. In her childhood also she was quite safe, in old age she was used to remain safest but in today's scenario a girl child is unsafe since her childhood till the end of her life. We listen daily about one or the other crime against female that can be rape of a girl child, of a young girl or of old women. Eve-teasing has also become a common problem. A girl is not safe even in home, what to talk about the school or workplace. This has become a serious problem and one of the main causes that today parents do not want to give birth to a girl child resulting into female foeticide which in turn reflected in declining juvenile sex ratio.

### *6.5.4 Crime Against Women*

If girl remains safe during her childhood and young age, parents look for a good family and a good bridegroom to settle their daughter's marriage. They marry their daughter with lots of wishes, blessings and gifts praying for her happy married life. But after some time, in many cases, parents face many problems and disappointment because her in-laws taunt her for her parent's status, many a times she is beaten by husband and in-laws and sometimes she is forced to suicide or is being burnt by them. This is also one of the major reasons for not wanting a girl child. By thinking about the future repercussions, they find it better not to give birth to a girl child instead of bowing down before others.

### *6.5.5 Negligence among Women about their Health*

In Haryana, most of the women are negligent about their health, they are busy in household chores right from the first ray of the sun, in Field Survey, in managing the animals, cleanliness of the house, cooking food for the family, washing clothes and in many other works. Moreover, if she is working women she had to cope with household and official works also. She is the one who has to take care of the health of all the family members, their necessities. She is busy in fulfilling wishes of all her family members' right from the morning till the end of the day. In this way, she always remains in hurry and had no time for herself. She neither cares for her food nor about her health. That is why, she is suffering from many of the diseases in all age groups basically female in Haryana are suffering from Anaemia. The data from NFHS-3 also substantiate this. Anaemia is a major health problem in Haryana, especially among women. Anaemia can result in maternal mortality, weakness, diminished physical and mental capacity, increased morbidity from infectious diseases, pre-natal mortality, premature delivery, low birth weight. Girls are more likely than boys to have anaemia. Children of mothers who have anaemia are much more likely to be anaemic. 56 per cent of women in Haryana have anaemia, including 38 per cent with mild anaemia, 17 per cent with moderate anaemia, and 2 per cent with severe anaemia. Anaemia is particularly high for women who are pregnant or breastfeeding and for women in the lowest wealth quintile.

## 6.6 Implications of Declining Juvenile Sex Ratio

Missing unborn girls because of female foeticide in Haryana has led to an alarming fall in male-female ratio. The situation has worsened since 1991, particularly in the 0-6 age-group. Census 2001 figures showed that the child sex ratio/juvenile sex ratio, which had become a concern in the 1991 census, has gone down even further—from 879 in 1991 to 820 in 2001 which is not a good sign for the future.

While in 1991, not a single district of Haryana recorded sex ratio less than 800, but in 2001, five districts namely Kurukshetra (771), Ambala (782), Sonipat (788), Kaithal (791), and Rohtak (799) recorded figures less than 800 girls per 1000 boys.

Out of the bottom ten districts in India in child sex ratio (CSR), Haryana alone accounts for 3 of them, with Kurukshetra (the pious land of Mahabharata) having the lowest—just 771 girls per 1000 boys (Table 6.11).

**Table 6.11:** Haryana: Child Sex Ratio in Bottom Ten Districts of India, 2001

| *Sr. No.* | *District* | *State* | *Child Sex Ratio* |
|---|---|---|---|
| 1. | Fathegarh Sahib | Punjab | 754 |
| 2. | Patiala | Punjab | 770 |
| **3.** | **Kurukshetra** | **Haryana** | **771** |
| 4. | Gurdaspur | Punjab | 775 |
| 5. | Kapurthala | Punjab | 775 |
| 6. | Bathinda | Punjab | 779 |
| 7. | Mansa | Punjab | 779 |
| 8. | Amritsar | Punjab | 783 |
| **9.** | **Sonipat** | **Haryana** | **783** |
| **10.** | **Ambala** | **Haryana** | **784** |

*Source*: Census of India (2001), *Provisional Population Totals,* Paper 1 of 2001 (Supplement), District Totals, Series-1, India, Statement-19, p. 46.

This imbalance in the sex composition of society may lead to disastrous demographic and social consequences for the state, e.g.:

- Perpetuation of crime against women;
- General rise in violence and crimes and worsening of law and order;
- Disturbances and imbalances at the family level and in interpersonal relationships;
- Female foeticide means *missing daughters* which, in turn, means *missing brides* for unemployed youth;
- Trafficking in girls as brides from backward states through the process of *buying and selling* of brides; and
- Female foeticide also accounts for a significant part of the decline in fertility.

**Table 6.12:** Haryana: Juvenile Sex Ratio of Target Villages (1st Stage)

| Sr. No. | State/ Tehsil | Village | Juvenile Sex Ratio (As per 2001 Census) | No. of House-holds | Sample Size (20%) | Juvenile Sex Ratio (As per Sample Survey) |
|---|---|---|---|---|---|---|
| | **Haryana** | | **819** | **25,41,980** | **11,357** | **722** |
| 1. | Panchkula | Barwala | 742 | 1,313 | 262 | 744 |
| 2. | Shahbad | Ismailabad | **678** | 2,184 | 436 | 724 |
| 3. | Kaithal | Habri | 732 | 1,897 | 378 | 722 |
| 4. | Karnal | Singoha | 742 | 1,014 | 202 | 869 |
| 5. | Israna | Naultha | 743 | 1,436 | 286 | 815 |
| 6. | Gohana | Dhanana Aladadpur | 724 | 1,087 | 216 | 842 |
| 7. | Kharkhoda | Rohna | **711** | 1,345 | 269 | 685 |
| 8. | Jind | Dauhla | 744 | 1,371 | 274 | 815 |
| 9. | Sirsa | Ding | 723 | 1,403 | 280 | 714 |
| 10. | Rania | Jiwan Nagar | 735 | 2,196 | 438 | 724 |
| 11. | Hisar | Satrod Kalan | 733 | 2,279 | 454 | 709 |
| 12. | Maham | Lakhan Majra | 749 | 1,641 | 328 | 810 |
| 13. | Rohtak | Hassangarh | 726 | 1,229 | 244 | 689 |
| 14. | Beri | Majra | 735 | 1,466 | 292 | 885 |
| 15. | Bahadurgarh | Badli | **716** | 2,608 | 520 | 842 |
| 16. | Jhajjar | Matanhail | 725 | 1,302 | 260 | 608 |
| 17. | Gurgaon | Kadipur (Part) | 745 | 1,677 | 334 | 803 |
| 18. | Palwal | Alawalpur | 750 | 1,235 | 247 | 710 |
| 19. | Palwal | Dhatir | 742 | 1,086 | 217 | 795 |
| 20. | Palwal | Janauli | 730 | 904 | 180 | 714 |
| 21. | Hodal | Pingor | 731 | 856 | 170 | 729 |
| | **Total Households** | | | **31,529** | **6,287** | |

*Source:* Census of India (2001) and Field Survey.

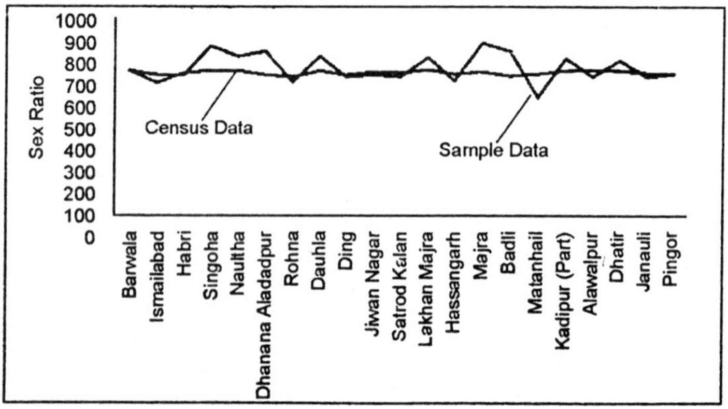


**Fig. 6.9:** Haryana: Juvenile Sex Ratio of Target Villages (1st Stage).

While analyzing the data of sample villages (Table 6.12 and Fig. 6.9), it is found that according to census data Ismailabad of Shahbad Tehsil in Ambala district was having the lowest sex-ratio (678 females per 1000 males) in the age-group 0-6. The main reason behind this was found that Ismailabad is now converted in a suburb of Ambala city, where diversification in economic activities is rapidly coming into existence with dominating male migration towards this place. However, the lowest sex-ratio in the villages surveyed in 1st stage is found in Matanhail of Jhajjar tehsil in the district of same name which is 608 females per 1000 males with an alarming decline of 117 points. Matanhail is in close proximity of city Jhajjar which is well linked by road network. It seems that the incidence of female foeticide is very much common in this area which has led to such a drastic result. According to sample survey, Matanhail is followed by Rohna village of Kharkhoda tehsil in Sonipat district with 685 females per thousand males and showing a decline of 26 points. Even as per 2001 census, Rohna was attributed with 2nd lowest sex-ratio that was 711 females per 1000 males. The 3rd lowest sex-ratio is found in Hassangarh village of Rohtak tehsil in the district of same name, where it is 689 females per 1000 males with a decrease of 37 points. In 2001 Census, the 3rd lowest sex-ratio in age-group 0-6 was depicted in Badli, where there were 716 females per thousand males but this village has shown very good results in terms of improvement of child sex-

**Table 6.13:** Haryana: Villages (1st Stage) with increase in Juvenile Sex Ratio (0-6) as per the Sample Survey

| *Village* | *Tehsil* | *Juvenile Sex Ratio (As per 2001 Census)* | *Juvenile Sex Ratio (As per Sample Survey)* | *Increase in Juvenile Sex Ratio (in points)* |
|---|---|---|---|---|
| Majra | Beri | 735 | 885 | 150 |
| Singoha | Karnal | 742 | 869 | 127 |
| Badli | Bahadurgarh | 716 | 842 | 126 |
| Dhanana Aladadpur | Gohana | 724 | 842 | 118 |
| Naultha | Israna | 743 | 815 | 72 |
| Dauhla | Jind | 744 | 815 | 71 |
| Lakhan Majra | Maham | 749 | 810 | 61 |
| Dhatir | Palwal | 742 | 795 | 53 |
| Ismailabad | Shahbad | 678 | 724 | 46 |
| Barwala | Panchkula | 742 | 744 | 2 |

*Source:* Field Survey.

ratio which has increased to 842 females per thousand males with an increase of 126 points. It seems that various health missionaries, *anganwadi* workers as well as social groups are successful in spreading the message in society that it is very important to maintain the sex-ratio to avoid the imbalance in sex components which can be harmful in future. The villages such as Majra (150 points), Singoha (127 points), Badli (126 points), Dhanana Aladadpur (118 points), Naultha (72 points), Dauhla (71 points), Lakhan Majra (61 points), Dhatir (53 points), Ismailabad (46 points), Barwala (2 points) have given encouraging results with increase in child sex ratio (Table 6.13 and Fig. 6.10).

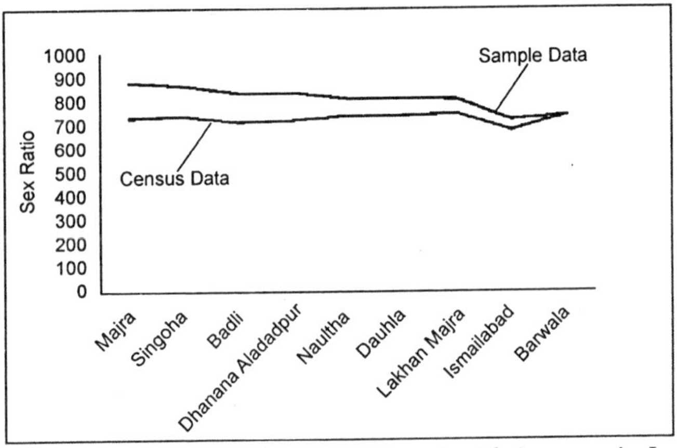


**Fig. 6.10:** Haryana: Villages (1st Stage) with increase in Juvenile Sex Ratio as per the Sample Survey

According to census 2001 data, Majra village in Naraingarh tehsil of Ambala district was having the lowest sex-ratio (597 females per 1000 males) in the age-group 0-6 (Table 6.14). But when the survey was done, it was encouraging to see that the sex ratio has increased and reached to the level of 686 females per 1000 males. The 2nd lowest village according to 2001 census data was Singanwala (Part) with 601 females per 1000 males, but this has reached to 734 females per 1000 males in the sample survey. It is followed by Lisan village which was having 3rd lowest juvenile sex ratio (604 females per 1000 males), but as per sample survey, it has reached to the level of 526 females per 1000 males, which is an alarming fall and needs great attention.

**Table 6.14:** Haryana: Juvenile Sex Ratio of Target Villages (2nd Stage)

| *Sr. No.* | *State/ Tehsil* | *Village* | *Juvenile Sex Sex Ratio (As per 2001 census)* | *No. of House-holds* | *Sample Size (20%)* | *Juvenile Sex Ratio (As per Sample Survey)* |
|---|---|---|---|---|---|---|
| | **Haryana** | | **819** | **25,41,980** | **11,357** | **722** |
| 1 | Panchkula | Garhi | 695 | 598 | 120 | 607 |
| 2 | Naraingarh | Kurali | 647 | 657 | 131 | 653 |
| 3 | Naraingarh | Majra | **597** | 740 | 148 | 686 |
| 4 | Ambala | Shahpur | 612 | 860 | 172 | 810 |
| 5 | Ambala | Singanwala (Part) | **601** | 763 | 152 | 734 |
| 6 | Shahbad | Jhansa | 694 | 1094 | 219 | 757 |
| 7 | Shahbad | Nalwi | 667 | 674 | 135 | 769 |
| 8 | Pehowa | Thaska Miranji | 688 | 697 | 139 | 750 |
| 9 | Guhla | Balbehra | 686 | 702 | 140 | 760 |
| 10 | Guhla | Kheri Gulamali | 651 | 624 | 125 | 717 |
| 11 | Kaithal | Sangri | 669 | 580 | 116 | 603 |
| 12 | Gharaunda | Phurlak | 682 | 586 | 117 | 672 |
| 13 | Gharaunda | Pabana Hassanpur | 666 | 562 | 112 | 750 |
| 14 | Panipat | Babail | 697 | 959 | 192 | 657 |
| 15 | Samalkha | Dehra | 685 | 688 | 137 | 896 |
| 16 | Sonipat | Nahri | 695 | 1244 | 249 | 785 |
| 17 | Sonipat | Barwasni | 665 | 865 | 163 | 607 |
| 18 | Sonipat | Karar Ibrahimpur | 632 | 616 | 123 | 712 |
| 19 | Kharkhoda | Bidhlan | 654 | 585 | 117 | 634 |
| 20 | Kharkhoda | Thana Kalan | 650 | 721 | 144 | 787 |
| 21 | Tohana | Pirthla | 696 | 630 | 126 | 682 |
| 22 | Sirsa | Rupawas | 670 | 537 | 107 | 677 |
| 23 | Sirsa | Darbi | 655 | 702 | 140 | 804 |
| 24 | Sirsa | Jhorar Nali | 639 | 938 | 188 | 864 |
| 25 | Sirsa | Nattar | 613 | 644 | 129 | 667 |
| 26 | Hisar | Sarsana | 692 | 265 | 53 | **533** |
| 27 | Bahadurgarh | Kharhar | 699 | 999 | 200 | 869 |
| 28 | Bahadurgarh | Jakhauda | 678 | 630 | 126 | 613 |
| 29 | Jhajjar | Machhrauli | 678 | 668 | 134 | 595 |
| 30 | Mahendragarh | Sehlang | 637 | 874 | 175 | 857 |
| 31 | Narnaul | Kanwariawas | 666 | 584 | 117 | **563** |
| 32 | Rewari | Dhawana | 686 | 633 | 127 | 600 |
| 33 | Rewari | Bharawas | 669 | 714 | 143 | 809 |
| 34 | Rewari | Lisan | **604** | 641 | 128 | **526** |
| 35 | Sohna | Rethoj | 700 | 545 | 109 | 824 |
| 36 | Hodal | Jatoli | 700 | 586 | 117 | 893 |
| | **Total Households** | | | **25,405** | **5,070** | |

*Source:* Census of India (2001) and Field Survey.

As far as the sample is concerned, the lowest juvenile sex ratio is in Lisan (526 females per 1000 males) followed by Sarsana (533 females per 1000 males) and Kanwariawas (563 females per 1000 males). These villages are showing the lowest sex ratio among the whole sample survey. It is a cause of worry that sex ratio has reached to about half of the male population. It will create a lot of social problems in the form of population imbalance, crime against women, trafficking of girls from other states as brides, increase in eve-teasing and rape cases, etc. All these are the abnormalities which can lead to drastic results.

On the contrary, there are villages (Jhorar Nali, Sehlang, Dehra) which have shown good results, where an increase of more than 200 points has been noticed. In Shahpur, Jatoli and Kharhar there is an increase of more than 170 points (Table 6.15 and Fig. 6.11).

**Table 6.15:** Haryana: Villages (2nd Stage) with increase in Juvenile Sex Ratio (0-6) as per the Sample Survey

| *Village* | *Tehsil* | *Juvenile Sex Ratio (As per 2001 Census)* | *Juvenile Sex Ratio (As per Sample Survey)* | *Increase in Juvenile Sex Ratio (in points)* |
|---|---|---|---|---|
| Jhorar Nali | Sirsa | 639 | 864 | 225 |
| Sehlang | Mahendragarh | 637 | 857 | 220 |
| Dehra | Samalkha | 685 | 896 | 211 |
| Shahpur | Ambala | 612 | 810 | 198 |
| Jatoli | Hodal | 700 | 893 | 193 |
| Kharhar | Bahadurgarh | 699 | 869 | 170 |
| Darbi | Sirsa | 655 | 804 | 149 |
| Bharawas | Rewari | 669 | 809 | 140 |
| Thana Kalan | Kharkhoda | 650 | 787 | 137 |
| Singanwala (Part) | Ambala | 601 | 734 | 133 |
| Rethoj | Sohna | 700 | 824 | 124 |
| Nalwi | Shahbad | 667 | 769 | 102 |
| Nahri | Sonipat | 695 | 785 | 90 |
| Majra | Naraingarh | 597 | 686 | 89 |
| Pabana Hassanpur | Gharaunda | 666 | 750 | 84 |
| Karar Ibrahimpur | Sonipat | 632 | 712 | 80 |
| Balbehra | Guhla | 686 | 760 | 74 |
| Kheri Gulamali | Guhla | 651 | 717 | 66 |
| Jhansa | Shahbad | 694 | 757 | 63 |
| Thaska Miranji | Pehowa | 688 | 750 | 62 |
| Nattar | Sirsa | 613 | 667 | 54 |
| Rupawas | Sirsa | 670 | 677 | 7 |
| Kurali | Naraingarh | 647 | 653 | 6 |

*Source:* Field Survey.

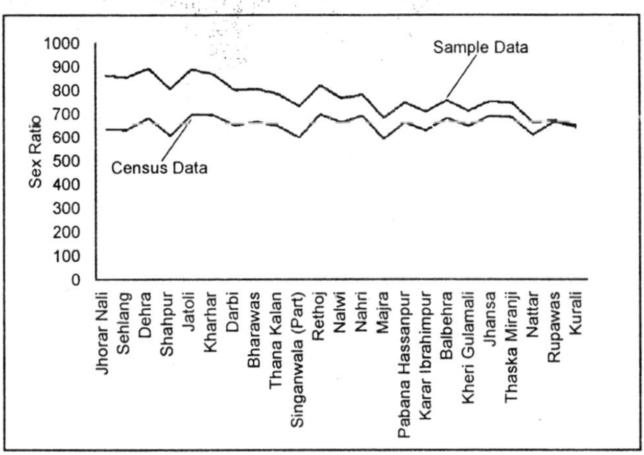


**Fig. 6.11:** Haryana: Villages (2nd Stage) with increase in Juvenile Sex Ratio (0-6) as per the Sample Survey.

Despite the fact that the juvenile sex ratio in Haryana has reached at an alarming level, people still do not prefer to have a family with a single daughter or daughters. Though, slow change in gender roles and expectations continues to take place, the responsibility of providing old age support for the parents lies on the son. Due to this expectation (9), major investments are being made in son(s), instead of daughter(s). The incidence of dowry is also increasing, despite the fact that juvenile sex ratio in some village has fallen drastically.

# 7 Conclusions, Strategies and Recommendations

## Conclusions

- The average size of household is smaller (5.0 persons per household) than the state as a whole (5.7 persons per household).
- The nuclear households comprise of 58.06 per cent and joint family system is prevalent among 41.94 per cent of the households. It means, the trend of joint family system is on the way of decline in the modern age of globalization.
- About 87 per cent head of the households are male, whereas only 12.7 per cent females are the head of the households, because most of them are widows. This shows that in the patriarchical society of Haryana, the household heads are predominantly males.
- There is hardly any *kachha* house inhabited by respondents selected from the target villages. Overall, the condition of more than 50 per cent sampled houses is good. This shows that people are liberal enough to expend money on their houses on the pattern of urban areas.
- About 94 per cent of the households in rural Haryana have electricity. With regard to water sources for drinking water, 95.4 per cent of the total households use drinking water from improved sources.
- More than half of the households (62 per cent) in rural Haryana have no toilet facility.

- Majority of the households are having all modern amenities for the comforts of life.
- In spite of all sort of development in Haryana, majority of the households (69.2 per cent) are still engaged in agricultural activities.
- About half (50.3 per cent) of the population is found in age group 15-44 and only 8.48 per cent are aged 60 or more.
- About 34.6 per cent of the population in Haryana is still illiterate. Among them, 49 per cent are females and 22.6 per cent are males.
- Only 30 per cent of women in Haryana have completed 10 or more years of education, compared with 44 per cent of men, indicating a wide gender disparity in literacy.
- The highest literacy rate is found in the tehsil of Gurgaon (77.28 per cent), whereas the lowest literacy rate is in Punahana tehsil (35.33 per cent).
- Punahana tehsil is also having the lowest literacy rate in terms of both male (53.65 per cent) and female (15.26 per cent) literacy, because of the dominance of Muslim population.
- The total literacy rate of the sampled population is 60.75 per cent in comparison to rural Haryana where total literacy rate is 63.19 per cent.
- Female literacy of sampled population is more (53.25 per cent) than the average of rural female literates (49.26 per cent) of Haryana. It shows the impact of awareness among women regarding education and the facilities provided to them by government in the form of free education up to graduation level as well as various incentives given to them in rural areas. One of the most important incentives to quote is the establishment of Mahila Vishwavidyalaya, Khanpur Kalan by the Government of Haryana basically to impart education to the girls of rural Haryana.
- A very noticeable feature of the society of Haryana is that all the respondents are of the opinion that some education must be imparted to both boys and girls. However, 53.7 per cent respondents believe that boys should be given as much education as they desire. On the contrary, only 36.5 per cent of respondents believe that a girl should be given as much education as she desires.

- Among the respondents, 56.9 per cent believe that girls should be married at the age of 18, whereas 55.8 per cent respondents feel that boys should not be married before 21 years of age. However, many of the boys and girls are being married before attaining the legal age of marriage. This is a common practice in villages but people do not complain against this because of harassments in legal processes. Moreover, this creates rivalry among their families.
- People are aware of legal age of marriage for boys and girls. They are reluctant enough to marry their children before the legal age of marriage whenever they find a suitable match. But they directly do not accept this truth. This in turn, increases teenage pregnancy and increasing incidence of foetal as well as maternal mortality rates.
- The infant mortality rate for Haryana— 42 per 1,000 live births—is much lower than the rate of 57 per 1,000 live births for India as a whole.
- Nearly 70 per cent of women say that boys and girls should get their mothers' feed for at least 12 months.
- Almost 90 per cent of the population in all age-groups has exposure to mass media. People get information and awareness through reading newspapers/magazine and watching TV.
- The perception of the majority of respondents (60.3 per cent) about ideal family size was two children. The ideal family composition as perceived by most of the respondents (58.7 per cent) includes one boy and one girl.
- About 60 per cent of the respondents feel *Dowry* is a major problem of the Society.
- Nearly 78 per cent respondents are of the opinion that marriage of a daughter has become a costlier affair which brings at least expenditure of 5 lakhs on one marriage.
- Most of the respondents were aware of the family planning practices and female *sterilization* is the most widely known method to limit the family size.
- Half of births (49 per cent) during the past five years took place with the assistance from a health professional, and another half of births were delivered by a traditional birth attendant.

- About 95 per cent respondents were not aware about the MTP Act and PNDT Act. But 92.1 per cent of the respondents were aware about the problem of declining juvenile sex ratio.
- Nearly 87 per cent respondents were aware of the places of sex determination tests. Though, they do not reveal whether they themselves had ever gone for such tests.
- Kurukshetra district, *the pious land of Mahabharata,* has the lowest sex ratio of 771 females per 1000 males. Kurukshetra district is followed by the districts of Ambala (782), Sonipat (788), Kaithal (791), and Rohtak (799) as per Census of India, 2001.
- Jind district has the highest rural-urban differential (+53) in the child sex ratio and is followed by the districts of Gurgaon (+50), Fatehabad (+36), Hisar (+33), Kaithal (+27), Panchkula (+26), Rohtak (+26), and Mahendragarh (+26).
- On the other hand, Faridabad district has the lowest rural-urban differential (+3) in the child sex ratio and is followed by the districts of Panipat (+3) and Kurukshetra (+6).
- The son preference is considered as the leading cause of declining juvenile sex ratio, because couples desire to have a male child for the continuation of their family tree, to support them in their old age and to perform last rituals.
- Female foeticide in Haryana has not only led to an alarming fall in male-female ratio, it has added many cruel dimensions to the nature of violence and crime and is even causing great disturbances and imbalances at the family level and in interpersonal relationships.
- The attitude of son preference is very much prevalent in the society of Haryana. Parents desire a male child:
    - For the continuation of their family tree.
    - To support them in their old age.
    - He is the earning partner.
    - To perform family rituals like performing funeral ceremony.
    - The girl is considered as *Praya Dhan,* because the female child grows and settles in her husband's household after marriage.
- The prevailing custom of early marriage of girls

particularly in rural areas brings in premature cohabitation and child-bearing resulting into high foetal and maternal mortality.

- In rural areas, frequent births during the reproductive age not only result in high maternal mortality rate but also reduce the life expectancy of the females in general.
- Unskilled mid-wifery especially in rural areas is also responsible for high maternal mortality rates.
- Miserable living condition of the females particularly in the lower-income groups is also one of the reasons for high female mortality rate particularly child-bearing age-group.
- Female foeticide is intrinsically linked to the dowry system in Haryana. Parents feel that girl is a burden. Expenditure on her education and marriage etc. drain their resources and are of no use for them. On the other hand, boys are thought to be earning hand, caretaker, performer of rituals, etc. So, investment on them can be cashed.
- The education level of female in Haryana is increasing, they are going outside home for jobs to earn money, yet only a small fraction of women indulge in the family decisions.
- A majority of respondents (74.3 per cent) were of the opinion that the decision to undergo sonography was taken by husband and in-laws.
- About 1/3rd of the respondents were anxious enough to know the sex of the foetus in the womb.
- About 70 per cent respondents were of the opinion that the maximum number of induced abortions in Haryana has taken place in private clinics.
- Among the respondents, the main cause for terminating pregnancy is for achieving the limited family size, basically which was not true.
- One of the basic reasons rooted in the thoughts of society for not wanting a girl child is the feeling of insecurity which is spreading in the form of a nuisance in the society. Crime against women is also responsible for declining sex ratio.
- Most of the women are negligent about their health, they are busy in household chores right from the first ray of the Sun, in managing the animals, cleanliness of the house,

cooking food for the family, washing clothes and in many other works. Anaemia is a major health problem in Haryana, especially among women which results in maternal mortality, weakness, diminished physical and mental capacity, increased morbidity from infectious diseases, pre-natal mortality, premature delivery, low birth weight.

- Missing unborn girls because of female foeticide in Haryana has led to an alarming fall in male-female ratio. This imbalance in the sex composition of society may lead to disastrous demographic and social consequences for the state, e.g.:
  - (i) Perpetuation of crime against women;
  - (ii) General rise in violence and crimes and worsening of law and order;
  - (iii) Disturbances and imbalances at the family level and in interpersonal relationships;
  - (iv) Female foeticide means *missing daughters* which, in turn, means *missing brides* for unemployed youth;
  - (v) Trafficking in girls as brides from backward states through the process of *buying and selling* of brides; and
  - (vi) Female foeticide also accounts for a significant part of the decline in fertility.
- It is interesting to note that the juvenile sex ratio in most of the target villages has increased as compared to the 2001 census data. Only a few villages are showing a decline in juvenile sex ratio, in comparison of the data obtained from Census of India, 2001.
- Impact of various schemes and policies of government (Janani Suraksha Yojna, Janani Suvidha Yojna, Ladli Yojna, Scholarship for single girl child, decrease in the age of old age pension for the parents of two daughters etc.) are somewhat visible in these villages.
- The role of NGOs, social reformer groups, social welfare groups as well as of various institutions is visible in the findings of field survey.
- Impact of mass media as well as of various advertisements and hoardings has also awakened the people in rural areas to increase sex ratio and not to go for sex determination tests.

- While analyzing the data of sample villages, it is found that according to Census of India (2001), Ismailabad village of Shahbad tehsil in Ambala district was having the lowest juvenile sex ratio (678 girls per 1000 boys). The main reason behind this was found that Ismailabad, at present, has developed as a suburb of Ambala city, where diversification in economic activities is rapidly coming into existence with dominating male migration towards this place.
- However, the lowest juvenile sex-ratio in the villages surveyed in first stage is found in Matanhail of Jhajjar tehsil which is 608 girls per 1000 boys with an alarming decline of 117 points. Matanhail is in close proximity of Jhajjar city which is well linked by road network. It seems that the incidence of female foeticide is very much common in this area which has led to such a drastic decline.
- Rohna village of Kharkhoda tehsil in Sonipat district with 685 girls per 1000 boys and showing a decline of 26 points is ranked second in terms of lowest juvenile sex ratio. Even as per 2001 census, Rohna was attributed with second lowest juvenile sex-ratio that was 711 girls per 1000 boys. The third lowest juvenile sex-ratio is found in Hassangarh village of Rohtak tehsil, where it is 689 girls per 1000 boys with a decrease of 37 points.
- One of the major findings of the present study is that an increase of more than 100 points in juvenile sex ratio has been noticed in the villages of Majra (150 points) of Beri tehsil, Singoha (127 points) of Karnal tehsil, Badli (126 points) of Bahadurgarh tehsil, and Dhanana Aladadpur (118 points) of Gohana tehsil.
- It seems that various health missionaries, *anganwadi* workers as well as social groups are successful in spreading the message in society that it is very important to maintain the juvenile sex ratio to avoid the imbalance in sex components which can be harmful for future generations.
- Lisan in Rewari tehsil with 604 girls per 1000 boys was at the third ranking in terms of lowest sex ratio, but but according to sample survey, the juvenile sex ratio in this

village has declined to the level of 526 girls per 1000 boys, which is an alarming fall and needs great attention.

- The other villages who follow the suite are Sarsana (533 girls per 1000 boys) in Hisar tehsil and Kanwariawas (563 girls per 1000 boys) in Narnaul tehsil. It is a cause of worry that juvenile sex ratio has reached to about half of the male population. It will create a lot of social problems in the form of population imbalance, crime against women, trafficking of girls from other states as brides, increase in eve-teasing and rape cases, etc. All these are the abnormalities which can lead to drastic results.
- On the contrary, there are villages like Jhorar Nali (225 points) in Sirsa tehsil, Sehlang (220 points) in Mahendragarh tehsil, and Dehra (211 points) in Samalkha tehsil) which have shown good results and where an increase of more than 200 points has been noticed in juvenile sex ratio. Similarly, the villages of Shahpur (198 points) in Ambala tehsil, Jatoli (193 points) in Hodal tehsil and Kharhar (170 points) in Bahadurgarh tehsil have experienced an increase of 170 points and more. This seems to be the result of efforts made by various social groups, government, mass media and the awareness about the adverse effects of the declining juvenile sex ratio.

## Strategies and Recommendations

The strategies and recommendations drawn on the basis of the findings of the present study are as follows:

(i) One possible way could be job reservation for women to take care of the financial stigma attached with them as daughters, because political empowerment, without economic empowerment, will not be enough.

(ii) A three-tier model for action involving the government, NGOs and Panchayati Raj Institutions (PRI), with technical back-up from academic experts, social activists and management experts should be adopted.

(iii) Local initiatives by NGOs and individuals with vision in such fields must be initiated.

(iv) Funds must be made available to organizations, especially in the health sector, to initiate an awareness campaign through the electronic and print media.

(v) A nation-wide campaign must be launched to recognize and spell out all forms of gender violence and the disastrous consequences of the demographic imbalance.

(vi) The role of the father in determining the sex of the child must be highlighted to counter the common perception that the mother is responsible in this matter.

(vii) All suspected cases of female foeticide must be examined by State Commissions and women's organizations, and action to punish erring doctors must be undertaken.

(viii) The government should consider empowering reputed NGOs to deal with cases of female foeticide on a trial basis. These can also be entrusted with the task of undertaking vigilance in suspected cases of SSAs.

(ix) The government should combine its population stabilization drive with measures to protect the girl child i.e. linking of population control measures to schemes for protecting the girl child with the slogan A*abaadi ghatao, beti bachao* (Reduce population, save the daughter).

(x) The PNDT and Dowry Acts must be implemented in letter and spirit. Existing loopholes should be plugged in the light of new technological developments and appropriate authorities set up under the Act should be more proactive in statutory laws like the MTP Act, 1992, and the PNDT Act, 1994 implementing their provisions.

(xi) There should be check on expenditures on the marriages because now-a-days it has become a costlier affair, people should follow the views of Swami Dayanand Saraswati and Swami Vivekanand which lies in *Arya Samaj*. According to the followers of these saints, marriages should be simple because it is a '*pavitra bandhan*' of two souls who are responsible for the progress of society. So all the ceremonies should be performed without pomp and show. There should be ban on the number of '*baraties*' and the *offerings* given by girls' parents.

# References and Bibliography


Agarwal, A. (2003), *Female Foeticide: Myth and Reality, 374 Case Histories of Woman who have undergone Female Foeticide*, Sterling Publishers, New Delhi.

Agarwal, S. and Unisa, S. (2010), "Active and Passive Elimination of Girl Child: Findings from Rural Haryana", in Sekher, T.V. and Hatti, Neelambar (eds.), *Unwanted Daughters: Gender Discrimination in Modern India*, Rawat Publications, Jaipur, pp. 222-243.

Agarwal, Sutapa (2005), "Discrimination from Conception to Childhood: A Study of Girl Child in Rural Haryana, India", *Draft Paper*, presented at CEPEDCICRED-INED seminar on Female Deficit in Asia: Trends and Perspectives, Singapore December 5-7, pp. 3-27.

Agnihotri, S.B. (1995), Missing Females: A Disaggregated Analysis, *Economic and Political Weekly*, Vol. 30(19), pp. 2074-84.

Agnihotri, S.B. (1996), Juvenile Sex Ratio in India: A Disaggregated Analysis, *Economic and Political Weekly*, Vol. 31, No. 52, pp. 3369-3382.

Agnihotri, S.B. (2000a), *Sex Ratio Patterns in the Indian Population: A Fresh Exploration*, Sage Publications, New Delhi.

Agnihotri, S.B. (2000b), "Rising Sons and Setting Daughters: Provisional Results of the 2001 Census", in Vina Mazumder and N. Krishnaji (eds.), *Enduring Conundrum: India's Sex Ratio: Essays in Honour of Asok Mitra*, Centre for Women's Development Studies, Rainbow Publishers, Delhi.

Alam, S.M. (1965), *Hyderabad and Secunderabad—Twin Cities: A Study in Urban Geography*, Allied Publishers Pvt. Ltd., New Delhi, pp. 77-93.

Anagol, P. (2002), "Women, Work and Abortion: A Case Study of Tamil Nadu", *Economic and Political Review*, Vol. 42 (12), pp. 1054-1059.

Arnold, Fred (1985), "Measuring the Effect of Sex Preference on Fertility: The Case of Korea, *Demography*, 22, pp. 280-288.

Arnold, Fred (1992), "Sex Preference and its Demographic and Health Implications", *International Family Planning Perspectives*, 18, pp. 93-101.

Arnold, Fred; Kishor, Sunita; and Roy, T.K. (2002), "Sex-Selective Abortions in India", *Population and Development Review*, Vol. 28 (4), pp. 759-785.

Arora, D. (1996), "The Victimizing Discourse: Sex Determination Technologies and Policy", *Economic and Political Weekly,* Vol. 31(7), pp. 420-424.

Balakrishnan, R. (1994), "The Social Context of Sex Selection and the Politics of Abortion in India", in Sen, Gita (ed.), *Power and Decision: the Social Control of Reproduction,* Harvard University Press, Cambridge, MA, pp. 267-286.

Bannerjee, N. (2002), "Between the Devil and the Deep Sea: Shrinking Option for Women in Contemporary India", in Kapadia, K. (ed.), *The Violence of Development: The Politics of Identity, Gender and Social Inequalities in India,* Zed Books, New York.

Bardhan, P. (1982), "Little Girls and Deaths in India", *Economic and Political Weekly,* Vol. 17, No. 36, 1982, pp. 1148-1150.

Basu, A. (1999), "Fertility Decline and Increasing Gender Imbalance in India, Including a Possible South Indian Turnaround", *Development and Change,* Vol. 30(2), pp. 237-263.

Bell, D.; Caplan, P.; and Karim, W. (eds.) (1993), *Gendered Fields: Women, Men and Ethnography,* Routledge, London.

Benston, M.L. (1992), "Women's Voices/Men's Voices: Technology as Language", in Kirkup, G. and Keeler, L.S. (eds.), *Inventing Women Polity,* Open University Press, London.

Bhalla, M. (2004), "The Land of Vanishing Girls: Sex Selective Abortion in Punjab", in Mohan Rao (ed.), *The Unbeard Scream: Reproductive Health and Women's Lives in India,* Zubaan, New Delhi.

Bhatnagar, R. and Dubey, R. (2005), *Female Infanticide in India: A Feminist Cultural History,* State University of New York Press, Albany.

Bhutani, S. (1995), *Demographic Dynamism in India,* Discovery Publishing House, New Delhi.

Billig, M. (1991), "The Marriage Squeeze on High–Caste Rajasthani Women", *Journal of Asian Studies,* Vol. 50(2), pp. 341-360.

Boling, P. (ed.) (1995), *Expecting Trouble: Surrogacy, Foetal Abuse, and New Reproductive Technologies,* Westview, Boulder, CO.

Borooah, G.L. (1985), *Population Geography of Assam: A Study of Dibrugarh District* (1872-1971), Mittal Publications, Delhi.

Bose, A. (1991), *Demographic Diversity of India: 1991 Census State and District Level Data,* B.R. Publishing Corporation, Delhi.

Bose, A. and Shiva, M. (2003), *Darkness at Noon: Female Foeticide in India,* Voluntary Health Association of India, New Delhi.

Bose, A. *et al.* (eds.) (1977), *Population Statistics in India,* Vikas Publishing House Pvt. Ltd., New Delhi.

Bower, L. (1995), "The Trope of the Dark Continent in the Foetal Harm Debates: Aricanism and the Right to Choice", in Patricia Boling (ed.), *Expecting Trouble: Surrogacy, Foetal Abuse, and New Reproductive Technologies,* Westview, Boulder, CO.

Bracken, H. and Nidaduvolu, V. (2005), "Mixed Messages: An Analysis of Communication Materials on Abortion and Sex Determination in Rajasthan", *Economic and Political Weekly*, 27, August, pp. 3856-62.

Bumiller, E. (1989), *May You Be the Mother of One Hundred Sons*, Ballantine, New York.

Bumiller, E. (1991), *May You Be the Mother of One Hundred Sons: A Journey among the Women of India*, Penguin Books, New Delhi.

Burgess, R. and Zhuang, J. (2000), *Modernisation and Son Preference*, Development Economics Discussion Paper, London School of Economics, London.

Byres, T.J. (1981), "Agrarian Structure, the New Technology and Class Action in India", *Journal of Peasant Studies*, Vol. 8, pp. 322-342.

Cain, M. (1994), *Women's Status and Fertility in Developing Countries: Son Preference and Economic Security*, World Bank Staff Working Papers, No. 682, Population and Development Series, No. 7.

Caldwell, J. (1982), *Theory of Fertility Decline*, Academic Press, London and New York.

Caldwell, J. and Caldwell, P. (1990), "Gender Implications for Survival in South Asia", *Health Transition Working Paper No. 7*, Australian National University, Canberra.

Caldwell, John C.; Reddy, P.H.; and Caldwell, Pat (1982), "The Causes of Demographic Change in Rural South India: A Micro Approach", *Population and Development Review*, Vol. 8, No. 4, pp. 689-727.

Census of India (1991), *Final Population Totals: Brief Analysis of Primary Census Abstract*, Paper 2 of 1992, Series-1, India, Office of the Registrar General and Census Commissioner, India, New Delhi.

Census of India (2001), *Final Population Totals*, Haryana, Series 7, Director of Census Operations, Haryana.

Census of India (2001), *Final Population Totals*, Series 1, India, Registrar General and Census Commissioner, New Delhi.

Census of India (2001), *Primary Census Abstract*, CDs 1-12, Office of the Registrar General and Census Commissioner, India, New Delhi.

Census of India (2001), *Primary Census Abstract*, Series-7, Haryana, Tables A5-A8, Director of Census Operations, Haryana, Chandigarh.

Census of India (2001), *Provisional Population Totals*, Paper 1 of 2001, Haryana, Series 7, Director of Census Operations, Haryana.

Census of India (2001), *Provisional Population Totals*, Paper 2 of 2001, Haryana, Series-7, Director of Census Operations, Haryana, Chandigarh, pp. 40-50.

Census of India (2011), *Provisional Population Totals*, Paper-1 of 2011, Haryana, Series 7, Director of Census Operations, Haryana.

Chandna, R.C. (1972), "Schedule Castes Population in Rural Haryana: A Geographic Analysis", *The National Geographical Journal of India*, 23, 3 and 4, pp. 177-186.

Chandna, R.C. (1986), *A Geography of Population: Concepts, Determinants and Patterns*, Kalyani Publishers, New Delhi.

Chandna, R.C. and Sidhu, M.S. (1979), "Sex Ratio and Its Determinants", *Transactions, Institute of Indian Geographers*, **1**, 1, pp. 17-23.

Chatterjee, Nillanjana and Riely, Nancy E. (2001), "Planning an Indian Modernity: the Gendered Politics of Fertility Control", *Journal of Women in Culture and Society*, Vol. 26, No. 3, pp. 811-845.

Chopra, R. (2004), "Encountering Masculinity: An Ethnographer's Dilemma", in Chopra, R.; Osella, C.; and Osella, F. (eds.) (2004), *South Asian Masculinities: Contexts of Change, Sites of Continuity*, Women Unlimited, New Delhi.

Chopra, R.; Osella, C.; and Osella, F. (eds.) (2004), *South Asian Masculinities: Contexts of Change, Sites of Continuity*, Women Unlimited, New Delhi.

Chunkath, S.R. and Athreya, V.B. (1997), "Female Infanticide in Tamil Nadu; Some Evidences", *Economic and Political Weekly*, 32(17), WS 21.

Clark, Shelley (2000), "Son Preference and Sex Composition of Children: Evidence from India", *Demography*, Vol. 37(1), pp. 95-108.

Clarke, J.I. (1960), "Rural and Urban Sex Ratios" *Tijdschrift voor Economische en Sociale Geografie*, **51**, p. 29.

Clarke, J.I. (1972), *Population Geography*, Pergamon Press, Oxford.

Coale, A. J. and Banister, J. (1994), "Five Decades of Missing Females in China", *Demography*, **31**, August, pp. 459-479.

Cooke, J. (2000), "Flexible Employment: Implications for a Gendered Political Economy of Citizenship", in Cooke, J.; Roberts, J.; and Waylen, G. (eds.), *Towards a Gendered Political Economy*, Macmillan, London.

Corbridge, S. and Harris, J. (2000), *Reinventing India*, Polity, Cambridge.

Corea, G., *et al.* (1985), *Man Made Women: How New Reproductive Technologies Affect Women*, Hutchinson, London.

Croll, Elisabeth (2000), *Endangered Daughters: Discrimination and Development in Asia*, Cup, Cambridge.

Croll, Elisabeth J. (2002), "Fertility Decline, Family Size and Female Discrimination: A Study of Reproductive Mismanagement in East and South Asia", *Asia-Pacific Population Journal*, **17**(2), pp. 11-38.

Dagar, R. (2001), *Combating Violence against Women in Punjab*, Institute for Development and Communication, Chandigarh.

Dagar, R. (2002), *Identifying and Controlling Female Foeticide and Infanticide in Punjab*, Institute for Development and Communication, Chandigarh.

Das Gupta, Monica (1987), "Selective Discrimination against Female Children in Rural Punjab, India", *Population and Development Review*, Vol. 13, No. 1, pp. 77-100.

Das Gupta, Monica (1995), "Fertility Decline in Punjab, India: Parallel with Historical Europe", *Population Studies*, Vol. 49, pp. 481-500.

Das Gupta, Monica and Mari Bhat, P.N. (1997), "Fertility Decline and

Increased Manifestation of Sex Bias in India", *Population Studies*, **51** (3), pp. 307-315.

Das Gupta, Monica; Zhenghua, Jing; Bohua, Li; Zhenming Xie; Chung, Woojin; and Hwa-Ok, Bae (2003), "Why is Son Preference so Persistent in East and South Asia? A Cross-Country Study of China, India and the Republic of Korea", *Journal of Development Studies*, Vol. 40, No. 2, pp. 153-187.

Dass, Maryan (1987), "Sex Preference and Fertility Behaviour: A Study of Recent Indian Data", *Demography*, 24(4), pp. 517-530.

Datamation Foundation, http:// indiafemalefoeticide. Org/, accessed on 21 January 2004.

Desai, P.B. (1967), "Variation in Population Sex-Ratios in India, 1901-61", in Bose, A. (ed), *Patterns of Population Change in India, 1951-61*, Allied Publishers, New Delhi, pp. 372-388.

Dubuc, S. and Coleman, D. (2007), "An Increase in the Sex Ratio of Births to India–born Mothers in England and Wales: Evidence for Sex–Selective Abortion", *Population and Development Review*, Vol. 33(2), June, pp. 383-400.

Dyson, T. (2001), "The Preliminary Demography of the 2001 Census of India", *Population and Development Review*, Vol. 27 (2), pp. 341-356.

Edlund, L. (1999), "Son Preference, Sex Ratios and Marriage Patterns", *Journal of Political Economy*, Vol. 107(6:1), December, pp. 1275-1304.

Elson, D. (1995), *Male Bias in the Development Process*, Manchester University Press, Manchester.

Feil, R.N., *et al.* (1984), "Attitudes Towards Abortion as a Means of Sex Selection", *Journal of Psychology*, Vol. 116(2), p. 271.

Forum Against Sex Determination and Sex Pre Selection (FASDSP) (1992), "Using Technology, Choosing Sex", *Development Dialogue 1 and 2*, pp. 91-92.

Franklin, S.H. (1956), "The Pattern of Sex Ratios in New Zealand, *Economic Geography*, **32**, pp. 162-176.

Ganatra, Bela; Hirve, Siddhi; and Rao, V.N. (2001), "Sex Selective Abortion: Evidence from a Community-based Study in Western India", *Asia-Pacific Population Journal*, Vol. 16, No. 2, pp. 109-124.

George, S.M. (1997), "Female Infanticide in Tamil Nadu: From Recognition Back to Denial?", *Reproductive Health Matters*, Vol. 10, November, pp. 124-132.

George, S.M. (2002), "Sex Selection/Determination in India: Contemporary Developments", *Reproductive Health Matters*, Vol. 10 (19), pp. 190-192.

George, S.M. and Dahiya, R.S. (1998), "Female Foeticide in Rural Haryana", *Economic and Political Weekly*, August 8, pp. 2191-98.

Gill, M. S. (2000), "Sex Ratio Differentials in Northwest India", *Population Geography*, **22**, 1 and 2, pp. 71-86.

Gill, M.S. and Singh, S.B. (1985), "Sex Ratio in Punjab, *Geographical Review of India*, **47**, 3, pp. 34-44.

Gilroy, F.D. and Steinbacher, R. (1991), "Sex Selection Technology Utilization: Further Implications for Sex Ratio Imbalance", *Social Biology*, Vol. 38(3-4), pp. 285-288.

Goel, N.P. (1994), *Readings in Population Geography*, Mohit Publications, New Delhi.

Goodkind, D. (1996), "On Substituting Sex Preference Strategies in East Asia: Does Pre-Natal Sex Selection Reduce Post-Natal Discrimination?", *Population and Development Review*, Vol. 22(1), pp. 111-125.

Gopalakrishnan, S. and Khanna, M. (2008), *A Socio-Cultural Study of the Declining Sex Ratio in Delhi and Haryana: A Report*, National Institute of Public Cooperation and Child Development, pp. 1-141.

Gosal, G.S. (1961), "The Regionalism of Sex Composition of India's Population", *Rural Sociology*, **26**, 2, pp. 122-137.

Gosal, R.P.S. (2001), "Sex Composition Analysis", *Population Geography*, **23**, 1 and 2, pp. 29-40.

Government of Haryana (2007), *Statistical Abstract of Haryana (2005-06)*, Economic and Statistical Advisor, Planning Department, Haryana.

Government of India (1996), "The Pre-Natal Diagnostic Techniques (Regulation and Prevention of Misuse) Act, 1994, *Gazetteer of India*, New Delhi.

Gulati, S.C. (1987), "Some Reflections on Son Preference and its Influence on Additional Desired Fertility", *Demography India*, 2, pp. 207-219.

Gulati, S.C. (1988), *Fertility in India: An Econometric Analysis of a Metropolis*, Sage Publications, New Delhi.

Gulati, S.K. and Nanda, A.K. (2011), "Declining Sex Ratio in a Prosperous Region: Economic Perspectives from Northern States of Haryana, Delhi, Punjab and Chandigarh", in Ram, F.; Unisa S. and Sekher, T.V. (eds.), *Population, Gender and Reproductive Health*, Rawat Publications, Jaipur, pp. 91-121.

Hanmer, J. (1985), "Transforming Consciousness: Women and the New Reproductive Technologies", in Gena Corea, *et al.* (eds.), *Man-Made Women: How New Reproductive Technologies Affect Women*, Hutchinsion, London.

Hassan, M.I. (2000), "Sex Composition of Haryana's Population: Some Evidences of Persisting Gender Inequality", *Man and Development*, **XXII**, 1, pp. 61-68.

Hassan, M.I. (2002), "Sex Ratio in Haryana's Population: A Disaggregated Spatial Analysis", *Geographical Review of India*, **64**,3, pp. 254-261.

Hatti, N.T.; Sekger, V.; and Larsen, M. (2004), "Lives at Risk: Declining Child Sex Ratio in India", *Lund Papers in Economic History*, No. 93.

Hatti, Neelambar and Ohalsson, Rolf (1984), "Age at Marriage: A Quantitative Study on Sirsi Taluk, 1960", *Demography India*, Vol. 13, No. 1, pp. 36-41.

Haughton, J. and Haughton, D. (1998), "Are Simple Tests of Son Preference Useful? An Evaluation using Data from Vietnam", *Journal of Population Economics*, Vol. 11, pp. 495-516.

Heyer, J. (1992), 'The Role of Dowries and Daughters", *Journal of International Development*, Vol. 4(4), pp. 419-436.

Hull, T. (1990), "Recent Trends in Sex Ratios at Birth in China", *Population and Development Review*, Vol. 16(1), pp. 3-83.

IIPS and Macro International (2007), National Family Health Survey (NFHS-3), 2005-2006: *India, International Institute for Social Sciences*, Mumbai.

Jayasree, R. and Audinarayana, N. (1991), "Differential Growth and Characteristics of Population Across the Ecological Regions of Tamil Nadu, 1991", *Demography India*, **20**, 1, pp. 35-40.

Jeffery, P. and Jeffery, R. (1996), *Don't Marry Me to Plowman: Women's Everyday Lives in Rural North India*, Westview, Boulder, Co.

Jeffery, R. and Jeffery, P. (1997), *Population, Gender and Politics: Demographic Change in Rural North India*, Cambridge University Press, Cambridge.

Jeffery, R.; Jeffery, P.; and Lyon, A. (1984), "Female Infanticide and Amniocentesis", *Social Science and Medicine*, Vol. 19(11), pp. 1207-1212.

Jha, Prabhatm; Kumar, Rajesh; Vasa, Priya; Dhingra, Neeeraj; Thiruchelvam, Deva; and Moineddin, Rahim (2006), "Low Male-Female Sex Ratio of Childern Born in India: National Survey of 1.1 Million Households, *The Lancet*, Vol. 367, pp. 211-218.

Johansen, S.; and Nygren, O. (1991), 'The Missing Girls of China, *Population and Development Review*, Vol. 17, pp. 35-51.

Johnston, H.B. (2002), *Abortion Practice in India: A Review of Literature*, CEHAT and Health Watch, May, Mumbai.

Junhong, C. (2001), "Prenatal Sex Determination and Sex Selective Abortion in Rural China", *Population and Development Review*, Vol. 27(2), pp. 259-281.

Kadi, A.S. (1987), "Age at Marriage in India, *Asia-Pacific Population Journal*, Vol. 2(1), March, pp. 41-56.

Kapadia, Karin (ed.), (2002), *The Violence of Development: The Politics of Identity, Gender and Social Inequalities in India*, Zed Books, New Delhi.

Kapur, M. (1998), *Difficult Daughters*, Penguin, New Delhi.

Kashyap, S.S. (1975), "The Changing Pattern of Sex-Ratio in Punjab", *Demography India*, **4**, 2.

Kaur, Ravinder (2010), "Across-Region Marriages: Poverty Female Migration and Sex Ratio", in Sekher, T.V. and Hatti, Neelambar (eds.), *Unwanted Daughters: Gender Discrimination in Modern India*, Rawat Publications, Jaipur, pp. 244-269.

Khanna, S.K. (1995), "Prenatal Sex Determination: A New Family-Building Strategy", *Manushi*, Vol. 86, pp. 23-29.

Khanna, S.K. (2001), "Shabri Jat and Dehati Jatni: The Indian Peasant Community in Transition", *Contemporary South Asia*, Vol. 10(1), pp. 37-53.

Khanna, S.K. (2009), *Fetal/Fatal Knowledge: New Reproductive Technologies and Family-Building Strategies in India*, Cengage/Wadsworth Publishing Company, Belmont, CA.

Khosla, T. (1980), "The Plight of Female Infants in India", *Journal of Epidemiology and Community Health*, pp. 143-146.

Kishor, Sunita (1993), May God Give Sons to All: Gender and Child Mortality in India, *American Sociological Review*, Vol. 58, April, pp. 247-65.

Kishor, Sunita (1995), "Gender Differentials in Child Mortality: A Review of Evidence" in Das Gupta, Monica; Lincoln Chen, C.; and Krishanji, T.N. (eds.) *Women's Health in India: Risk and Vulnerability*, Oxford University Press, Bombay.

Kishwar, M. (1995), "When Daughters are Unwanted: Sex Determination Tests in India", *Manushi*, Vol. 86, pp. 15-22.

Krishan, G. and Chandna, R.C. (1973), "Sex Composition of Haryana's Population", *Geographical Review of India*, **35**, 2, pp. 113-125.

Krishnaji, N. (2001), "The Sex Ratio Debate", in Mazumdar, Vina and Krishnaji, N. (eds.) (2002), *Enduring Conundrum: India's Sex Ratio: Essays in Honour of Ashok Mitra*, Centre for Women's Development Studies, Rainbow Publishers, Delhi, pp. 28-35.

Krishnaji. N. (1987), "Poverty and Sex Ratio", *Economic and Political Weekly*, 22, 23, pp. 892-97.

Kumar, Dharma (1983), "Male Utopias or Nightmares?" *Economic and Political Weekly*, Vol. 18(3), January 15, pp. 61-64.

Kumudini Dandekar (1975), "Why has the Proportion of Women in India's Population been Declining", *Population and Development Review*, 13(1), pp. 77-100.

Kundu, Amitabh and Sahu, M.K. (1991), "Variation in Sex Ratio: Development Implications", *Economic and Political Weekly*, Vol. 26, No. 41, pp. 2341-2342.

Lahiri, S. (1984), "Demand for Sons among Indian Couples by Urban-Rural Settlement Size", *Demography India*, 13(1), pp. 120-132.

Lal, H. (1987), *City and Urban Fringe: A Case Study of Bareilly*, Concept Publishing Co., New Delhi.

Lall, A. (1962), "Age and Sex Structure of Cities of India", *Geographical Review of India*, **24**, 1, pp. 7-29.

Larsen, Mattisa; Hatti, Neelambar; and Gooch, Pernille (2005), "Uncertainty and Discrimination: Family Structure and Declining Child Sex Ratios in Rural India", Lund Paper in Economic History, *Population Economics*, No. 99.

Larsen, Mattisa; Hatti, Neelambar; and Gooch, Pernille (2010), "Inter-Generational Interests, Uncertainity and Discrimination: Declining

Child Sex Ratio in India", in Sekher, T.V. and Hatti, Neelambar (eds.), *Unwanted Daughters: Gender Discrimination in Modern India,* Rawat Publications, Jaipur, p. 8.

Lingam, L. (1998), "We:Sex Detection Tests and Female Foeticide: Discrimination before Birth", in Lingam, L. (ed.), *Understanding Women's Health Issues: A Reader,* Kali for Women, New Delhi.

Malhotra, A. (2002), *Gender, Caste and Religious Identities: Restructuring Class in Colonial Punjab,* Oxford University Press, New Delhi.

Malhotra, A. (2005), "The Pativrata and Domestic Ideologies in Early Twentieth Century Punjab", in Kak, S. and Pati, B. (eds.), *Exploring Gender Equations: Colonial and Postcolonial India,* Nehru Memorial Museum and Library, New Delhi.

Mallik, R. (2002), "Sex Selection: A Gender-Based Preference for a Pregnancy", *Reproductive Health Matters,* Vol. 10 (19), pp. 189-190.

Mari Bhat, P.N. (2000), "On the Trail of 'Missing Indian Females, 1: Search for Clauses, Special Articles", *Economic and Political Weekly,* Dec. 21, pp. 5105-18.

Mari Bhat, P.N. (2002), "On the Trail of Missing Indian Females, II: Illusion and Reality", *Economic and Political Weekly,* December 28, pp. 5244-63.

Mari Bhat, P.N. and Francis Zavier, A.J. (2003), "Fertility Decline and Gender Bias in Northern India", *Demography,* Vol. 40, No. 4, pp. 637-657.

Mari Bhat, P.N. and Francis Zavier, A.J. (2007), Factors Influencing the Use of Prenatal Diagnostic Techniques and Sex Ratio at Birth in India, in Attane, I. and Guilmoto, C.Z. (eds.), *Watering the Neighbour's Garden: the Growing Demographic Female Deficit in Asia,* Committee for International Cooperation in National Research in Demography, Paris.

Mari Bhat, P.N. and Francis Zavier, A.J. (2010), "Factors Influencing the Use of Prenatal Diagnostic Techniques and the Sex Ratio at Birth in India", in Sekher, T.V. and Hatti, Neelambar (eds.), *Unwanted Daughters: Gender Discrimination in Modern India,* Rawat Publications, Jaipur, pp. 104-139.

Mari Bhat, P.N.; Preston, Samuel; and Dyson, Tim (1984), *Vital Rates in India 1961-1981,* National Academy Press, Washigton, D.C.

Maurya, S.D. and Devi, G. (1985), "Changing Pattern of Urban Sex Ratio in Uttar Pradesh", *National Geographer,* **20**, 2, pp. 171-182.

Mazumdar, Vina and Krishnaji, N. (eds.) (2002), *Enduring Conundrum: India's Sex Ratio: Essays in Honour of Ashok Mitra,* Centre for Women's Development Studies, Rainbow Publishers, Delhi.

McNeil, M., Varcoe, I. and Yearly, S. (1990), *The New Reproductive Technologies,* Macmillan, London.

McNicoll, Geofffrey and Cain, Mead (1989), "Institutional Effects on Rural Economic and Demographic Change", *Population and Development Review,* Vol. 15, Supplement: Rural Development and Population: Institutions and Policy, pp. 3-42.

Mehta, S. and Kaur, G. (1983), "Rural-Urban Differences in Sex Ratio of Rajasthan", *The Indian Geographical Journal*, **58**, 2, pp. 152-161.

Menon, N. (1998), "The Impossibility of Justice: Female Foeticide and Feminist Discourse on Abortion", in Uberoi, P. (ed.), *Social Reform, Sexuality and the State*, Sage, London.

Michael, A. Koening and Stan D' Souza (1987), "Sex Differences in Childhood Mortality in Rural Bangladesh", *Social Science and Medicine*, 22 (1), pp. 15-22.

Miller, B.D. (1981), *The Endangered Sex: Neglect of Female Children in Rural North India*, Cornell University Press, Ithaca, NY.

Miller, B.D. (1989), "Changing Patterns of Juvenile Sex Ratios in Rural India, 1961-1971", *Economic and Political Weekly*, Vol. 24, No. 22, pp. 1229-36.

Mishra, U.; Ramathan, S.; and Rajan, S. (1998), "Induced Abortion Potential among Indian Women", *Social Biology*, Vol. 45 (3/4), pp. 278-288.

Misra, B.D. (1980), *An Introduction to the Study of Population*, South Asian Publishers Pvt. Ltd., New Delhi.

Mitra, A. (1979), *Implications of Declining Sex-Ratio in India's Population*, Allied Publishers Pvt. Ltd., New Delhi, pp. 1-85.

Mohanty, Chandra (1991), *Third World Women and the Politics of Feminism*, Indiana University Press, Bloomington, IN.

Momsen, J.H. and Townsend, J.G. (eds.) (1987), *Geography of Gender in the Third World* (State University of New York Press, 1987)

Mumtaj Begam and Singh, Christianna (2010), "Status of the Girl Child and Son Preference in Mumbai", in Sekher, T.V. and Hatti, Neelambar (eds.), *Unwanted Daughters: Gender Discrimination in Modern India*, Rawat Publications, Jaipur, pp. 11-12.

Muthuayappa, R.; Choe, M.K.; Arnold, F.; and Roy, T.K. (1997). "Son Preference and its Effect on Fertility in India", *National Family Health Survey, Subject Report*, No 3, March, International Institute for Population Sciences, Mumbai.

Narinder Uberoi Kelly (1975), *Some Socio-Cultural Correlates of Indian Sex Ratios: Case Studies of Punjab and Kerala*, Unpublished Doctoral Dissertation, University Press, Ithaca.

Nath, V. (1991), *Official Paper on 1991 Census, Economic Development*, Allen and Unwin, London.

Natrajan, D. (1971), Change in Sex Ratio, *Census Centenary Monograph*, No. 6, New Delhi, Officer of the Registrar General.

Nayar, Usha (1995), *Doomed before Birth: Study of Declining Sex Ratio in the Age Group 0-6 Years in Selected Districts of Punjab and Haryana*, NCERT, Department of Women's Studies, New Delhi, p. 287.

Nayar, Usha. (2006), *The Unborn Daughters of Delhi*, The Women Press, Delhi.

NFHS-3, Haryana State Report, 2008.

Office of the Deputy Commissioner of Nawanshahr District (2005), *The Nawanshahr Model*, Report on the Anti- Feticide Campaign.

Oldenburg, P. (1992), 'Sex Ratio, Son Preference and Violence in India: A Research Note, *Economic and Political Weekly*, Vol. 27(49/50), 5-12 December, pp. 2657-62.

Osella, C. and Osella, F. (2006), *Men and Masculinities in South India*, Anthem Press, London.

Padmanabha, (1982), "Mortality in India: A Note on Trends and Implications", *Economic and Political Weekly*, 17,32, pp. 1285-1290.

Pandey, G. (1990), *The Construction of Communalism in Colonial North India*, Oxford University Press, Delhi.

Panigrahi, L. (1972), *British Social Policy and Female Infanticide in India*, Munshiram Manoharlal, Delhi.

Patel, T. (1994), *Fertility Behaviour: Population and Society in a Rajasthan Village*, Oxford University Press, Delhi.

Patel, T. (ed.), (2007), *Sex-Selective Abortion in India: Gender, Society and New Reproductive Technologies*, Sage Publications, New Delhi.

Patel, Tulsi (2010), "Risky Lives: Indian Girls Caught Between Individual Rationality and Public Good", in Sekher, T.V. and Hatti, Neelambar (eds.), *Unwanted Daughters: Gender Discrimination in Modern India*, Rawat Publications, Jaipur, pp. 16-37.

Patel, V. (1988), "Sex Determination and Sex Pre-Selection Tests: Abuse of Advanced Technologies", in Ghadially, Rehana (ed.), *Women in Indian Society*, Sage Publications, New Delhi, pp. 178-85.

Patel, V. (1989), Sex Determination and Sex Pre-Selection Tests in India: Modern Techniques for Femicide, *Bulletin for Concerned Asian Scholars*, Vol. 21(1), January-March.

Pauline Kolenda (1987), *Regional Differences in Family Structure in India*, Rawat Publications, Jaipur.

Perianayagam, A. (2005), "Sex Ratio at Birth and Excess Female Child Mortality in India", *Draft Paper*, presented at CEPEDCICRED-INED seminar on Female Deficit in Asia: Trends and Perspectives, Singapore December 5-7, 2005.

Prakasam, C.P. (2010), "Imbalance in Sex Ratio in Rural Tanil Nadu: A Case study of Salem District", in Sekher, T.V. and Hatti, Neelambar (eds.), *Unwanted Daughters: Gender Discrimination in Modern India*, Rawat Publications, Jaipur, p. 10.

Prasad, R. (1990), *Population Geography of India: A Case Study of Rajasthan*, Radha Publications, New Delhi.

Prasad, Shweta (2001), "Female Foeticide: A Study of Varanasi", Centre for Women's Studies and Development, Lucknow, p. 14.

Pravin M. Visaria (1969), The Sex Ratio of the Population of India, Census of India, 1961, Vol. I, *Monograph No.10*, Ministry of Home Affairs, Office of the Registrar General, New Delhi.

Premi, M.K. (2001), "The Missing Girls Child", *Economic and Political Weekly*, 26, May, 1875-1880.

Premi, M.K. and Raju, Saraswati (1992), "Decline in Sex Ratio: Alternative Explanation Re-examined", *Economic and Political Weekly*, Vol. 27(17), April 25, pp. 911-912.

Punjab Lok Sujag (2005), *Missing Millions: Sex Ratio Differences in Pakistan and Gender Profile of Okara and Pakpattan Districts*, Punjab Lok Sujag, Lahore.

Purewal, N. (2003), "Reproducing South Asian Women: Female Foeticide and the Spectacle of Culture", in Puwar, N. and Raghuram, P. (eds.), *South Asian Women in the Diaspora*, Berg, Oxford.

Purewal, N. (2004), "Sex-Selection and Feminist Internet-Works", *Journal of Inter-Disciplinary Gender Studies*, pp. 103-119.

Puri, J. (1999), *Women, Body, Desire in Post Colonial India: Narratives of Gender and Sexuality*, Routledge, New York.

Rajan, S. Irudaya; Mishra, U.S.; and Navaneetham, K. (1991), "Decline in Sex Ratio: An Alternative Explanation", *Economic and Political Weekly*, December 21, pp. 2963-2964.

Rajarretnam, T. (1995). "Family Size Desire, Sex Preference, Socio-Economic Condition and Contraceptive Use in Rural Karnataka, India", *Demography India*, 24(2), pp. 275-290.

Rajput, P. (2004), *A Situational Analysis of Women and Girls in Punjab*, National Commission for Women, New Delhi.

Raju, K.N.M. and Bhat, T.N. (1995), "Sex Composition of Living Children against Socio-Economic Variables while Accepting Family Planning Methods", *Demography India*, Vol. 24, No. 1, pp. 87-99.

Ramu, G.N. (1988), *Family Structure and Fertility: Emerging Patterns in an Indian City*, Sage Publications, New Delhi.

Randeria, S. and Visaria, L. (1984), "Sociology of Bride-Price and Dowry", *Economic and Political Weekly*, 19(15), 14 April, pp. 648-652.

Rao, V. (1993), "The Rising Price of Husbands: A Hedonic Analysis of Dowry Increases in Rural India", *Journal of Political Economy*, Vol. 101 (4), pp. 666-667.

Ravindra, R.P. (1985), Myths About Sex Determination Tests", *Facts Against Myths*, 2(3), June, Vikas Adhyayan Kendra, Mumbai, pp. 1-6.

Ravindra, R.P. (1987), "Struggle Against Sex Determination Techniques: Unfinished Battle", *Economic and Political Weekly*, Vol. 22(12), pp. 490-492.

Raymond, J.G. (1993), *Women as Wombs: Reproductive Technologies and the Battle over Women's Freedom*, Harper Collins, San Francisco.

Reddy, M.M.K. (1996), *An Introduction to Demographic Behaviour in India*, Kanishka Publishers, New Delhi, pp. 53-70.

Registrar General and Census Commissioner of India (2003), *Missing: Mapping the Adverse Child Sex Ratios in India*, Office of Registrar General and Census Commissioner of India.

Registrar General of India (2005), *Special Fertility and Mortality Survey, 1988: A Report of 1.1 Million Indian Households,* Registrar General, New Delhi.

Retherford, R.D. and Roy, T.K. (2003), "Factors affecting Sex-Selective Abortion in India and 17 Major States", *National Family Health Survey Reports,* No. 21, IIPS, Mumbai, and East-West Centre, Hawaii.

Retherford, R.D. and Roy, T.K. (2003), Factors Affecting Sex Selective Abortion in India, *National Family Health Survey Bulletin,* 17, January, IIPS, Mumbai and East West Center, Hawaii.

Samaiyar, Priyajit and Joe, William (2010), "Implications of Declining Sex Ratio on Marriage Squeeze of India", in Sekher, T.V. and Hatti, Neelambar (eds.), *Unwanted Daughters: Gender Discrimination in Modern India,* Rawat Publications, Jaipur, p. 12.

Sangari, K. and Vaid, S. (eds.) (1990), *Recasting Women: Essays in Indian Colonial History,* Rutgers University Press, New Brunswick, NJ.

Sangwan, R.S. and Sangwan, Sneh (2008), "Unborn Girls in Haryana: Evidence from the Field", *Population Geography,* Vol. 30, Nos. 1&2, pp. 91-101.

Sangwan, Sneh and Sangwan, R.S. (2003), *Rural-Urban Divide: Changing Spatial Pattern of Social Variables,* Concept Publishing Company, New Delhi, pp. 100-125.

Santalahti, P., Hemmiki, E., Latikka, A. and Rynanen, M. (1998), Women's Decision-Making in Prenatal Screening", *Social Science and Medicine,* Vol. 46(8), pp. 1967-76.

Sarna, K. (2003), "Female Feticide on the Rise in India", *Nursing Journal of India.*

Scrimashaw, N.S. and Gleason, G.R. (1992), *Rapid Assessment Procedures: Qualitative Methodologies for Planning and Evaluation of Health Related Programmes,* International Nutrition Foundation for Developing Countries (INFDC), Boston, MA, USA.

Sekher, T.V. and Hatti, Neelambar (2007). "Vulnerable Daughters in a Modernizing Society: From Son Preference to Daughter Discrimination in Rural South India", in Attane, Isabelle and Guilmoto, C.Z. (eds.), *Watering the Neighbours' Garden: The Growing Demographic Female Deficit in Asia,* Committee for International Cooperation in National Research in Demography, Paris (CICRED), Paris.

Sekher, T.V. and Hatti, Neelambar (eds.) (2010), *Unwanted Daughters: Gender Discrimination in Modern India,* Rawat Publications, Jaipur, pp. 10-11.

Sekher, T.V.; Hatti, Neelambar; and Bhat, Preethi (2010), "From Fertility Control to Gender Control: Evidences of Gender Discrimination in Rural South India", in Sekher, T.V. and Hatti, Neelambar (eds.), *Unwanted Daughters: Gender Discrimination in Modern India,* Rawat Publications, Jaipur.

Sen, A. (1990), "More Than 100 Million Women are Missing", *New York Review of Books*, 20 December, pp. 61-66.

Sen, Amartya and Sunil Sengupta (1983), "Malnutrition of Rural Children and the Sex Bias", *Economic and Political Weekly*, 18, 19, 20, 21, pp. 855-864.

Sen, S. (2002), "The Savage Family: Colonialism and Female Infanticide in Nineteenth Century India", *Journal of Women's History*, Vol. 14(3), pp. 53-79.

Senapati, R.N. (1993), "Sex-Ratio: Trends and Implications in India", *Vision*, **13**, 1 and 2, pp. 92-100.

Sharma, U. (1980), *Women, Work and Property in North-West India*, Tavistock, London.

Sharma, U. (2005), "Dowry in North India: Its Consequences for Women", in Basu, S. (ed.), *Dowry and Inheritance*, Women Unlimited, New Delhi.

Sheel, R. (1999), *The Political Economy of Dowry: Institutionalization and Expansion in North India*, Manohar, New Delhi.

Shyrock, H.S. (ed.) (1976), *The Method and Materials of Demography*, Academic Press, New York, p. 105.

Siddhanta, S.; Nandy, D.; and Agnihotri, S.B. (2003), "Sex Ratio and Prosperity Effect: What do NSSO Data Reveal?", *Economic and Political Weekly*, Vol. 38(41), p. 4381.

Siddiqui, F.A. (1982), "Regional Analysis of the Sex-Structure of Population of Uttar Pradesh", *The National Geographical Journal of India*, **28**,1 and 2, pp. 74-85.

Siddiqui, F.A. and Ahmad, Q.M. (1971), "Regional Variation of the Sex-Ratio in the Population of Haryana", *The Geographer*, **18**, pp. 99-114.

Singh, N.G.K. (2009), "Female Foeticide in the Punjab and Foetus Imagery in Sikhism, in Sasson, V.R. and Law, J.M. (eds.), *Imagining the Foetus: The Unborn in Myth, Religion and Culture*, Oxford University Press, New York.

Singh, P. (1983), "Dowry among Jat Sikhs in Punjab", *How*, Special Dowry Number, May, Delhi.

Sinha, V.C. (1979), *Dynamics of India's Population Growth*, National Publishing House, New Delhi.

Snehi, Y. (2003), "Female Infanticide and Gender in Punjab: Imperial Claims and Contemporary Discourse", *Economic and Political Weekly*, 11 October, pp. 4302-4305.

Spallone, P. (1997), "Technologies of Reproduction: Why Women's Issues Make a Difference", in Maynard, M. (ed.), *Science and the Construction of Women*, UCL Press, London.

Srinivas, M.N. (2005), "Some Reflections on Dowry", in Basu, S. (ed.), *Dowry and Inheritance*, Kali for Women and Women Unlimited, New Delhi.

Srivastava, Arti; Dasgupta, Papia; and Rai, Shashi (2005), *Attitude towards Girl Child and Declining Sex Ratio in Bhopal,* Centre for Women's Studies, Bhopal, p. 42.

Sudha, S. and Rajan, S. Irudaya (1999), "Female Demographic Disadvantage in India 1981-1991: Sex-Selective Abortions and Female Infanticide", *Development and Change,* 30 (2), pp. 585-618.

Sudha, S.; Khanna, Sunil; Irudaya Rajan, S.; and Srivastava, Roma (2010), "Traditions in Transformation: Emerging Son Preference Attitudes among the Nairs of Kerala", in (2009) in Unwanted Daughters: Gender Discrimination in Modern India Eds.: T.V. Sekher and N. Hatti, Jaipur and New Delhi: Rawat Publications, India.

Susan, C. and Scrimshaw, M. (1978), "Indian Mortality and Behaviour in the Regulation of Family Size", *Population and Development Review,* Vol. 4(3), pp. 383-403.

Swaminathan, M.; Mangai, A.; and Raja, Samuel S. (1998), *Comforting Discrimination: Some Approaches to the Issue of Female of India,* New Delhi.

Trewartha, G.T. (1953). "A Case for Population Geography", *Annals of the Association of American Geographers,* 43, p. 51.

Unisa, Sayeed; Pujari, S. and Usha, R. (2007), "Sex Selective Abortions in Haryana: Evidence from Pregnancy History and Prenatal Care", *Economic and Political Weekly,* 42(1), pp. 60-66.

Unisa, Sayeed; Sinha, R.K.; Prakasam, C.P. (2002), *"Sex Selective Abortions in India: Evidence from two Cultural Settings"*, Paper presented at symposium on sex ratio in India, organised by IIPS, 10-11 January, 2002.

Unisa, Sayeed; Sinha, R.K.; Prakasam, C.P. and Bhagat, R.B. (2003), *"Evidence of Sex Selective Abortions from two Cultural Settings of India A Study of Haryana and Tamil Nadu"* Unpublished Report, International Institute for Population Sciences, Mumbai.

United Nations Population Fund India (2001), *Sex Selective Abortions and Fertility Decline: The Case Study of Haryana and Punjab,* Published Report, September, 2001.

Visaria, Leela (2002), "Deficit of Women in India: Magnitude, Trends, Regional Variations and Determinants", *The National Medical Journal of India,* 15(1), pp. 19-25.

Visaria, Leela (2007), "Sex Selection Abortion in Gujarat and Haryana: Some Empirical Evidence", in Visaria, Leela and Ramachandran, Vimala (eds.), *Abortion in India: Ground Realities,* Routledge, New Delhi, pp. 133-167.

Visaria, P. (1971), The Sex Ratio of the Population of India, Census of India 1961, *Monograph No. 10,* Office of the Registrar General of India, New Delhi.

Vishawanath, L.S. (1996), "Female Infanticide and the Position of Women in India", in Shah, A.M.; Baviskar, B.S.; and Ramaswamy, E.A. (eds.),

*Social Structure and Change*, Vol. 2: *Women in Indian Society*, Sage Publications, New Delhi, pp. 179-202.

Vishawanath, L.S. (2000), *Female Infanticide and Social Structure: A Socio-Historical Study in Western and Northern India*, Hindustan Publishing, New Delhi.

Vishawanath, L.S. (2004) "Female Infanticide: The Colonial Experience", *Economic and Political Weekly*, 29 May, pp. 2313-18

Visveswaran, K. (1994), *Fictions of Feminist Ethnography*, University of Minnesota Press, London.

Winch, R.F. (1964), *The Modern Family*, Holt Rinehart and Winston, New York.

Wyon, Johns B. and Gordon, John E. (1971), *The Khanna Study: Population Problems in the Punjab*, Harvard University Press, Massachusetts, Cambridge.

Yadav, S.S. and Badri, V.S. (1997), *Gender Preference and Anxiety of Pregnant Women*, Bangalore, Population Centre, pp. 10-14.

# Index